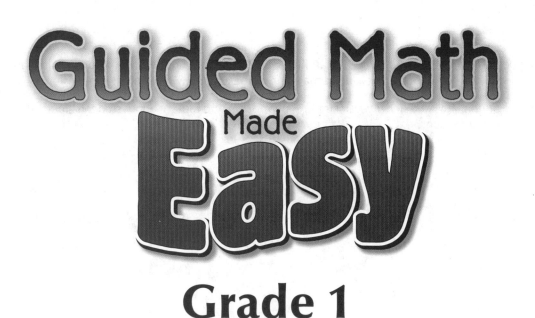

# Guided Math Made Easy

## Grade 1

by Margaret Burkholder

D1500796

Carson-Dellosa Publishing LLC
Greensboro, North Carolina

**Caution:** Before beginning any nature activity, ask families' permission and inquire about students' plant and animal allergies. Remind students not to touch plants or animals during the activity without adult supervision.

**Caution:** Before beginning any food activity, ask families' permission and inquire about students' food allergies and religious or other food restrictions.

# Credits

Content Editor: Amy R. Gamble
Copy Editor: Rebecca Benning
Layout Design: Van Harris
Cover Design: Lori Jackson

This book has been correlated to state, common core state, national, and Canadian provincial standards. Visit *www.carsondellosa.com* to search for and view its correlations to your standards.

Carson-Dellosa Publishing LLC
PO Box 35665
Greensboro, NC 27425 USA
www.carsondellosa.com

ISBN 978-1-60996-468-9
01-335111151

# Table of Contents

# Skills Matrix

| Page Numbers | Addition | Subtraction | Counting | Sorting | Compare & Order | Patterns | Money | Measurement | Time | Geometry | Data Analysis & Probability | Problem Solving |
|---|---|---|---|---|---|---|---|---|---|---|---|---|
| 6–9 | ● | | ● | | | ● | | | | | | ● |
| 10–13 | ● | | ● | | | | ● | | | | | ● |
| 14–17 | ● | | ● | | | | | | | | | ● |
| 18–21 | ● | | ● | | | ● | | | | | | ● |
| 22–25 | | | ● | | | ● | | | | | | ● |
| 26–29 | ● | | ● | | | ● | ● | | | | | ● |
| 30–33 | | | | | | ● | | | | | | ● |
| 34–37 | ● | ● | | | | | | | | | | ● |
| 38–41 | ● | ● | | | | | | | | | | ● |
| 42–45 | ● | ● | | | | ● | | | | | | ● |
| 46–49 | | | | | ● | | | | | | | ● |
| 50–53 | ● | ● | | | | ● | | | | | | ● |
| 54–57 | | | ● | | ● | | | ● | | | | ● |
| 58–61 | | | | | ● | | | ● | | | | ● |
| 62–65 | | | | | ● | | | | ● | | | ● |
| 66–69 | | | | | ● | | | | | ● | | ● |
| 70–73 | | | | ● | ● | | | | | ● | | ● |
| 74–77 | | | | ● | ● | | | | | ● | | ● |
| 78–81 | | | | | ● | | | | | ● | | ● |
| 82–85 | | | | ● | | | | | | | ● | ● |
| 86–89 | | | ● | ● | ● | | | | | | ● | ● |
| 90–93 | | | | | | | | | | | ● | ● |

CD-104542 © Carson-Dellosa

# Introduction

One of the most challenging aspects of teaching mathematics is differentiating instruction to meet the needs of all of the learners in your classroom. As a classroom teacher, you are responsible for teaching the state and district standards to mastery by the end of the school year. But, the reality inside the classroom is that for some students the material is too difficult, while for others the material is too easy. In the reading classroom, many teachers use guided reading groups as an excellent way to teach to the various levels of readers. In a small-group setting, teachers are able to monitor the progress of students and vary instruction according to need.

This book provides a resource for using the same approach in the math classroom. The lessons are intended to supplement your existing curriculum by providing ideas for differentiated instruction. Throughout the year, refer to the lessons and activity sheets in *Guided Math Made Easy* to introduce topics, provide additional practice, or expand on learning.

*Guided Math Made Easy* is organized by the five National Council of Teachers of Mathematics (NCTM) content strands: Number and Operations, Algebra, Measurement, Geometry, and Data Analysis & Probability. Specific objectives were chosen from each strand to cover the areas with which first graders usually have the most difficulty or need additional classroom support.

A teacher resource page is provided for each objective. On these pages, mini-lessons are presented first. Mini-lessons are intended for whole-group instruction to introduce each concept. Next, you will find three differentiated group lessons. Group 1 Lesson is for below-level learners, Group 2 Lesson is for on-level learners, and Group 3 Lesson is for above-level learners. These hands-on group lessons can be used after each mini-lesson to practice or reinforce the skill. For below-level learners, group lessons can be used as pre-teaching lessons to introduce each topic.

After each teacher resource page, three activity sheets are provided—one for each level of learner. These sheets can be used for review, sent home for homework, placed at a center, or used for informal assessments.

## Key

Below Level: ◯

On Level: ☐

Above Level: △

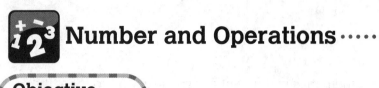

# Number and Operations

## Objective
Count items in a set.

**Materials:**
- Collection of classroom objects (e.g., pens, books, flags, paper clips)
- 1 die
- Spoon
- Container of dried beans
- Glue
- Construction paper
- Math notebooks
- Activity sheets (pages 7–9)

## Mini-Lesson

1. Students should be able to recognize up to 10 objects quickly without mistakes. This skill can help them count larger sets of objects.
2. Encourage students to find sets of classroom objects with 1–10 items in each set. For example, 1 teacher, 2 flags, 3 windows, etc.
3. Share the sets of objects students identify and write the object names on the board. For example, "1 teacher," "2 flags," "3 windows," etc. Ask, "How many sets have only one object? What about sets of two? Three? What is the largest set in the classroom?"
4. Show students a die. Ask, "Why are these numbers easy to recognize without counting? Can you arrange the sets in ways that make them easier to count?" Encourage students to discover different arrangements.

## Group 1 ○

**Recognizing Small Numbers**
1. Draw a set of 6 stars on the board in 2 columns of 3. Ask students to tell the number of stars without counting. Ask, "How can we quickly recognize the number of stars in this set?"
2. Show students other number patterns using a die or other star arrangements on the board as examples.
3. Have each student use a spoon to scoop a small amount of beans from the container. Students should guess the number of beans they have by looking at them, not by counting.
4. Instruct students to draw or glue the beans onto construction paper in some order (lines or groups) that will help them quickly recognize the number.
5. Ask students to write a reflection in their math notebooks answering the prompt, "What method can I use to quickly count objects?"

## Group 2 □

**Group to Count**
1. Draw 25 stars in sets of 5 (arranged as on a die) on the board. Ask students to guess how many stars there are and how they decided on their answers.
2. Encourage students to explore the strategy of counting by looking for sets of 2s, 3s, 5s, or 10s.
3. Have students reach into a container of beans and grab a handful. Challenge them to count the beans several times, grouping them by 2s, 3s, 5s, or 10s.
4. Have students draw or glue their beans onto construction paper in groupings that they feel are best for counting. Ask, "How did you group your beans? What did you do with the leftover beans that did not fit into a new group?"
5. Ask students to write a reflection in their math notebooks answering the prompt, "How can grouping objects help me count quickly?"

## Group 3 △

**Estimate and Check**
1. Have students draw a three-column chart in their math notebooks labeled *My Guess*, *Beans*, and *My Count*.
2. Have each student reach into the container of beans and grab a handful.
3. Without looking, have each student estimate how many beans she is holding. Then, have her record her guess in the first column of her chart.
4. Next, have students draw their beans onto the chart in the second column. Encourage students to group the beans for quick counting.
5. Have students count and record the actual number in the last column of the chart.
6. Repeat with more handfuls. Ask, "Did your estimates get better after more tries? Why?"
7. Ask students to write a reflection in their math notebooks answering the prompt, "How did you estimate how many beans you could hold in your hand?"

Name_____

Write the number shown.

1.

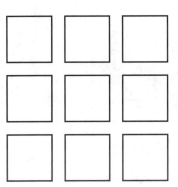

_____

2.

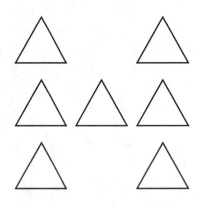

_____

3.

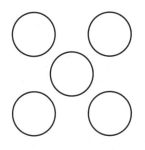

_____

4.

_____

Follow the directions to draw circles.

5. Show 12 circles grouped by 2s.

6. Show 18 circles grouped by 3s.

7. Show 25 circles grouped by 5s.

8. Show 20 circles grouped by 4s.

Name_____

Count each group of objects by circling smaller, equal groups.
Write the number of objects shown.

1.
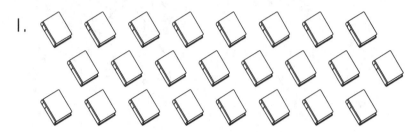

_____

2.
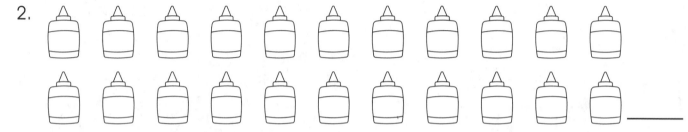

_____

3.
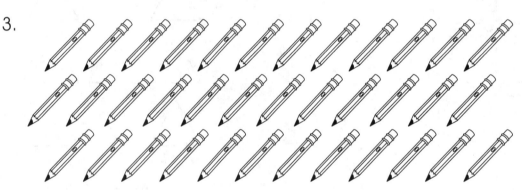

_____

Draw the correct number of dots to follow each counting pattern.

4. Count to 20 by 2s.

5. Count to 35 by 5s.

6. Count to 50 by 10s.

Name_____

Estimate the number of objects in each group. Then, circle smaller groups to count.

1.

Estimate: _____

Actual: _____

2.

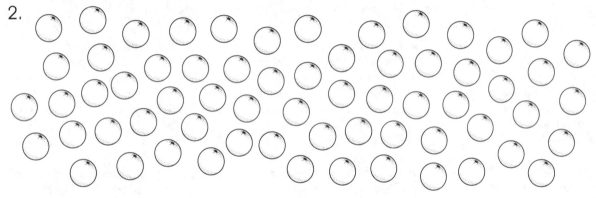

Estimate: _____

Actual: _____

3.

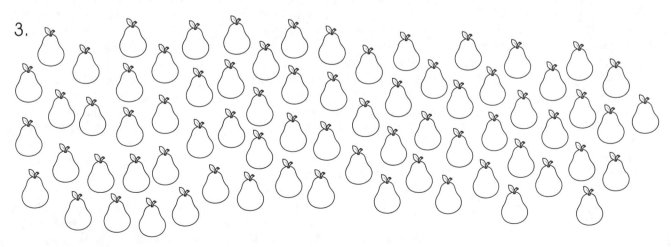

Estimate: _____

Actual: _____

**Number and Operations** ·········

## Objective
Count and group objects in ones and tens.

**Materials:**
- Straws
- Rubber bands
- Pennies and dimes
- Math notebooks
- Collection of classroom objects (e.g., pens, books, flags, paper clips)
- Price tags
- Paper
- Activity sheets (pages 11–13)

## Mini-Lesson

1. Ask students what they know about tens and ones. Explain that 10 ones are in 1 ten. Ask students to think of things that come in 10s (e.g., fingers and toes).
2. Line up 10 students and give each a high-five with both hands, counting to 100 by 10s. Ask, "How many students do we need to count to 50? How many tens are in 50?"
3. Line up 10 different students. Tap each of their fingers with your thumb. Count to 100 by 1s. Ask, "How many students do we need to count to 100? How many ones are in 100?"
4. Combine counting with hands and thumbs by giving high-fives with both hands and thumb taps to count to 45 (10, 20, 30, 40, 41, 42, 43, 44, 45). Explain that tens and ones are added together to make a variety of two-digit numbers.

## Group 1 ○

**Making Tens**
1. Demonstrate grouping by 10s and adding on 1s by bundling straws. Distribute between 11 and 19 straws to each student and have them count the number of straws.
2. Have students count 10 straws and bind them with a rubber band. Now, have them count the straws again. Ask, "How did you count differently with and without the straws bundled? Which way was easier?"
3. Give each student a handful of pennies. Have them count by making stacks of 10. Ask, "How many stacks of 10 make 50¢? How many stacks of 10 do you need to make $1.00?"
4. Ask students to write a reflection in their math notebooks answering the prompt, "How does grouping and counting by 10s help us?"

## Group 2 □

**Dimes and Pennies**
1. Model counting tens and ones using dimes and pennies. For example, 45¢ is 4 dimes and 5 pennies. Count aloud as you lay out the coins: "10, 20, 30, 40, 41, 42, 43, 44, 45."
2. Provide each student with a handful of dimes and pennies and a variety of classroom objects with price tags marked 99¢ or less.
3. Have students count the money needed to purchase each classroom object. Help students count dimes first, by 10s, then pennies, by 1s. If appropriate, allow each student to purchase an object of their choosing with the correct coin combination.
4. Encourage students to trade stacks of 10 pennies for additional dimes. Ask, "How many pennies equal 1 dime? How many dimes are in 73¢?"
5. Ask students to write a reflection in their math notebooks answering the prompt, "How do pennies and dimes relate to place value?"

## Group 3 △

**Adding Tens and Ones**
1. Provide each student with a handful of pennies and dimes. Challenge students to count the coins using tens and ones. Remind students not to use more than 9 pennies. Ask them to explain why.
2. Set out a variety of objects and label with prices of 99¢ or less.
3. Have each student choose two items and record the prices on a "receipt" sheet of paper. Then, have students calculate the total cost. At the bottom of their receipts, have students write the number of dimes and pennies needed for their purchases.
4. Ask, "What would we need to exchange 10 dimes for to show a total of more than 99¢?" You may wish to provide dollar bills to extend the lesson and work with making change.
5. Ask students to write a reflection in their math notebooks answering the prompt, "Today, we shopped with just pennies and dimes. What was the easiest part? What was the hardest part?"

Name_____

## Write how many tens and ones to model each number.

1. 12

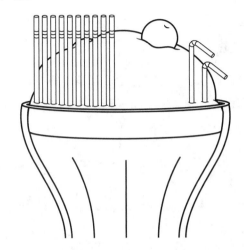

_____ ten _____ ones

2. 6

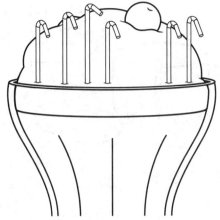

_____ tens _____ ones

3. 21

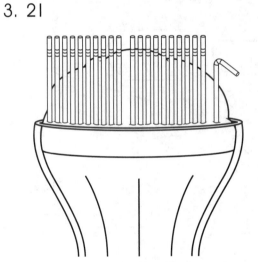

_____ tens _____ one

4. 19

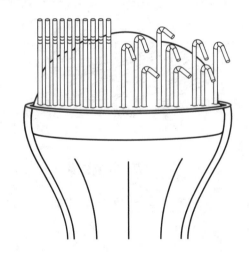

_____ ten _____ ones

5. 34

_____ tens

_____ ones

6. 70

_____ tens

_____ ones

7. 57

_____ tens

_____ ones

8. 42

_____ tens

_____ ones

9. 63

_____ tens

_____ ones

10. 95

_____ tens

_____ ones

Name_____

Write how many dimes and pennies you need to purchase each snack item.

1.
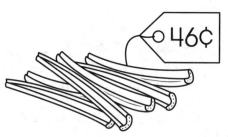 83¢

_____ dimes

_____ pennies

2.
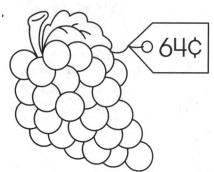 64¢

_____ dimes

_____ pennies

3.
 59¢

_____ dimes

_____ pennies

4.
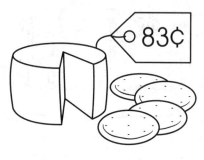 46¢

_____ dimes

_____ pennies

5.
 87¢

_____ dimes

_____ pennies

6.
21¢

_____ dimes

_____ penny

7.
38¢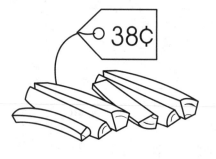

_____ dimes

_____ pennies

8.
 70¢

_____ dimes

_____ pennies

9.
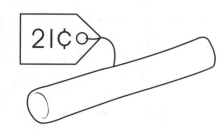 93¢

_____ dimes

_____ pennies

Name_____

Write how many dimes and pennies you need to purchase each set of items. Show your work.

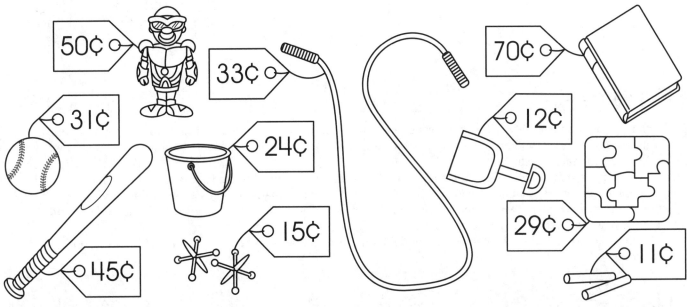

50¢    31¢    33¢    24¢    70¢    12¢    29¢    11¢    15¢    45¢

1. Bat and ball

   Total cost: _____

   _____ dimes

   _____ pennies

2. Action figure and jump rope

   Total cost: _____

   _____ dimes

   _____ pennies

3. Ball and jacks

   Total cost: _____

   _____ dimes

   _____ pennies

4. Jump rope and chalk

   Total cost: _____

   _____ dimes

   _____ pennies

5. Pail and shovel

   Total cost: _____

   _____ dimes

   _____ pennies

6. Book and puzzle

   Total cost: _____

   _____ dimes

   _____ pennies

7. Puzzle and jacks

   Total cost: _____

   _____ dimes

   _____ pennies

8. Book and action figure

   Total cost: _____

   _____ dimes

   _____ pennies

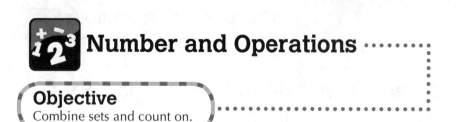

# Number and Operations

**Materials:**
- Printed number lines (0–20)
- Counters
- Math notebooks
- 6-sided and 10-sided dice
- Activity sheets (pages 15–17)

## Objective
Combine sets and count on.

## Mini-Lesson

1. Practice counting from 0 to 12 by calling students to the front of the classroom. Have students count aloud with you as you start with no one (0) up front. Count as you call up 1 student, then another (2), and another (3), until you reach 12 students.
2. Have students sit and call 5 different students to the front of the room. Ask students to count how many classmates are standing up front. Now, call up 3 more. Ask, "How many students are up front now? What was your strategy for finding the answer?" Some may count from 1 to 8, others may start with 5 and add on, and others may use their math facts to add 5 + 3.
3. Demonstrate each of these strategies and model them on a number line as you count the students again together.

## Group 1 ○

### Comparing Methods
1. Ask students to model 6 + 2 using counters. Have them count 6 counters in one group and 2 counters in another group, then add by counting the total by 1s to 8.
2. Show students how to use a number line to count on, sharing that it is faster than starting from zero. Ask students to model 6 + 2 using number lines. Have each student place a counter at 6 on the number line, then add by moving the counter along the number line 2 times to 8.
3. Let students practice using both methods with a variety of facts.
4. Ask, "What is the difference between adding using a number line and adding using counters? Which do you prefer? Why?"
5. Ask students to write a reflection in their math notebooks answering the prompt, "What is one method for adding two numbers?"

## Group 2 □

### Counting On and the Commutative Property
1. Have each student roll a 6-sided die and mark that number with a counter on a number line. Direct students to roll the dice again and count on to add that many more to the marked number. They may point to each number as they count on or move the counter to each number to find the answer.
2. Ask students to write the problem as a number sentence. Then, have them write the same problem with the addends in a different order and model the new equation on their number lines. Ask, "Is the answer still the same? Which number is easier to start with? Why?"
3. Let students practice with a variety of facts.
4. Ask students to write a reflection in their math notebooks answering the prompt, "How do you add on a number line?"

## Group 3 △

### Counting On and Back
1. Have each student roll a 10-sided die and mark that number with a counter on a number line.
2. Direct students to roll the dice again and count on to add that many more to the marked number. Then, ask them to count back to subtract that many and return to the marked number.
3. Ask students to write both problems as number sentences. Let students practice with a variety of facts. Ask students to share their number sentences and model them on a number line for the group.
4. Ask, "How is a number line used for adding? How can you use the counting on strategy for subtraction? How are your addition and subtraction number sentences related?"
5. Ask students to write a reflection in their math notebooks answering the prompt, "How are adding and subtracting on a number line the same? How are they different?"

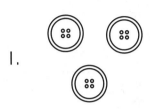
Name_____

## Add to write the total number of objects.

1. 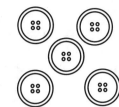 + = _____

2. + = _____

3. + = _____

4. + = _____

## Count on the number line to add. The starting point is marked for you. Circle your answer.

5. 5 + 3

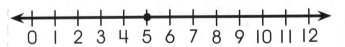

6. 7 + 4

7. 2 + 8

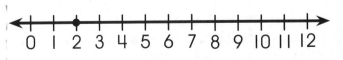

8. 0 + 7

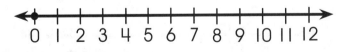

9. 6 + 6

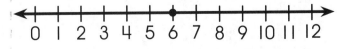

10. 12 + 0

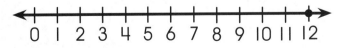

Name_____

Roll a number cube once for each number line. Count on to add that amount. The starting point is marked for you. Circle your answer. Then, write the same problem in another way.

1. 8 + _____ = _____

   _____ + _____ = _____

2. 9 + _____ = _____

   _____ + _____ = _____

3. 12 + _____ = _____

   _____ + _____ = _____

4. 7 + _____ = _____

   _____ + _____ = _____

5. 6 + _____ = _____

   _____ + _____ = _____

6. 1 + _____ = _____

   _____ + _____ = _____

7. 10 + _____ = _____

   _____ + _____ = _____

8. 14 + _____ = _____

   _____ + _____ = _____

**16**

Name_____

Roll a number cube once for each number line. Count on to add that amount. The starting point is marked for you. Circle your answer. Then, count back to subtract that amount. Write an addition and subtraction sentence.

1. 8 + _____ = _____

_____ − _____ = _____

2. 9 + _____ = _____

_____ − _____ = _____

3. 12 + _____ = _____

_____ − _____ = _____

4. 7 + _____ = _____

_____ − _____ = _____

5. 6 + _____ = _____

_____ − _____ = _____

6. 1 + _____ = _____

_____ − _____ = _____

7. 10 + _____ = _____

_____ − _____ = _____

8. 14 + _____ = _____

_____ − _____ = _____

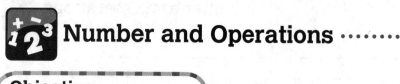

# Number and Operations

Materials:
- Balls
- Math notebooks
- Hundred charts
- Crayons
- Counters
- Activity sheets (pages 19–21)

## Objective

Count by 2s, 5s, and 10s to 100.

## Mini-Lesson

1. Have students stand in a row and call out one by one to count by 1s.
2. Say, "You can also count by other amounts. This makes counting things faster. Let's try counting by 2s." Count the number of feet in the line, counting by 2s.
3. Ask, "By what numbers can we count our fingers?" Have each student hold up one hand. Count the number of fingers in the line, counting by 5s. Then, have each student hold up both hands. Count the number of fingers in the line, counting by 10s.
4. Discuss other things that can be counted by 2s, 5s, and 10s.

## Group 1 ○

**Skip Counting Game**

1. Let students practice skip counting by 2s, 5s, and 10s to 100. If students struggle, encourage them to whisper the numbers they would skip.
2. Have pairs of students play catch and count. Each time a player catches the ball, she should call out a number the pair skip counts by 2s, 5s, or 10s.
3. Ask, "If you and your partner toss the ball a total of 3 times counting by 10s, what number will you count to? How many times will you and your partner toss the ball to count to 25 if you count by 5s?" Let students answer these questions by tossing the ball and counting.
4. Ask students to write a reflection in their math notebooks answering the prompt, "What is skip counting?"

## Group 2 ☐

**Skip Counting on the Hundred Chart**

1. Give each student a hundred chart and crayons.
2. Instruct students to skip count by 2s and color those blocks yellow, by 5s and color those blocks red, and by 10s and color those blocks blue.
3. Encourage students to look at the patterns. Ask, "What kind of numbers are yellow? Are any numbers all 3 colors? Are there any red numbers that aren't also yellow or blue?"
4. Ask students to write a reflection in their math notebooks answering the prompt, "What is skip counting? What patterns did you see in the colorful hundred chart?"

## Group 3 △

**Start on a Different Number**

1. Give each student a hundred chart and crayons.
2. Instruct students to skip count by 2s starting at 2 and color those blocks yellow, then skip count by 2s starting at 1 and color those blocks blue. Ask, "What are the yellow numbers called? What are the blue numbers called?"
3. Give each student another hundred chart and some counters. Let students experiment with counting by 5s and 10s starting at different numbers. Ask, "What numbers will you count if you start on 7 and count by 10s? If you count by 5s starting at 3, will you include 18?"
4. Encourage students to predict patterns when counting by 3s, 4s, or 9s, then mark numbers with counters on the hundred charts and describe the patterns.
5. Ask students to write a reflection in their math notebooks answering the prompt, "What is skip counting useful for?"

Name_____

Follow the directions to skip count. Write the missing numbers.

1. Count by 2s.

   2, _____ , _____ , 8, _____ , _____ , _____ , _____ , _____ , 20

2. Count by 5s.

   5, _____ , _____ , _____ , 25, _____ , _____ , _____ , _____ , 50

3. Count by 10s.

   10, _____ , _____ , _____ , _____ , 60, _____ , _____ , _____ , 100

4. Count by 2s.

   _____ , _____ , 24, _____ , 28, _____ , _____ , _____ , 36, _____

5. Count by 5s.

   _____ , 35, _____ , _____ , _____ , _____ , 60, _____ , _____ , _____

6. Count by 10s.

   _____ , _____ , 50, _____ , _____ , _____ , _____ , _____ , _____ , 120

Skip count to write the missing numbers. Then, write the number you skip counted by.

7. Count by _____ .

   74, _____ , _____ , _____ , 82, _____ , _____ , 88, _____ , _____

8. Count by _____ .

   _____ , 20, _____ , _____ , _____ , 40, _____ , _____ , 55, _____

Name_____

Follow the directions to skip count. Write the missing numbers.

1. Count by 2s.

2, _____ , _____ , _____ , _____ , _____ , _____ , _____ , _____ , _____

2. Count by 5s.

5, _____ , _____ , _____ , _____ , _____ , _____ , _____ , _____ , _____

3. Count by 10s.

10, _____ , _____ , _____ , _____ , _____ , _____ , _____ , _____ , _____

4. Count by 2s.

_____ , _____ , 56, _____ , _____ , _____ , _____ , _____ , _____ , _____

5. Count by 5s.

_____ , _____ , _____ , 70, _____ , _____ , _____ , _____ , _____ , _____

6. Count by 2s.

1, _____ , _____ , _____ , _____ , _____ , _____ , _____ , _____ , 19

7. Count by _____ .

_____ , _____ , 30, _____ , _____ , _____ , _____ , _____ , 60, _____

Name_____

Follow the directions to skip count. Write the missing numbers.
Then, answer the questions.

1. Skip count by 2s.

   20, _____ , _____ , _____ , _____ , _____ , _____ , _____ , _____ , _____ , 40

   Are these numbers even or odd? _____

2. Skip count by 2s.

   5, _____ , _____ , _____ , _____ , _____ , _____ , _____ , _____ , _____ , 25

   Are these numbers even or odd? _____

3. Skip count by 5s.

   4, _____ , _____ , _____ , _____ , _____ , _____ , _____ , _____ , _____

4. Skip count by 10s.

   _____ , _____ , 28, _____ , _____ , _____ , _____ , _____ , _____ , _____

5. Skip count by 3s.

   3, _____ , _____ , _____ , 15, _____ , _____ , _____ , _____ , _____

6. Skip count by 4s.

   4, _____ , _____ , _____ , 20, _____ , _____ , _____ , _____ , _____

7. Skip count by 2s from 6 to 42. Skip count by 3s from 6 to 42. Which
   numbers do you count in both of the sets?

   _____

8. Skip count by 3s from 30 to 120. Skip count by 5s from 30 to 120. Skip count
   by 10s from 30 to 120. Which numbers do you count in all of the sets?

   _____

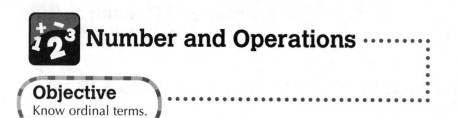

# Number and Operations

**Objective**
Know ordinal terms.

**Materials:**
- First-, second-, and third-place ribbons
- Crayons
- Stapler and staples
- Math notebooks
- Activity sheets (pages 23–25)

## Mini-Lesson

1. Introduce ordinal numbers and explain that they name the position of an object, such as *first, second,* and *third.*
2. Encourage students to suggest everyday uses of ordinals: street names, instructions, awards, etc.
3. Arrange students in three teams and hold an ordinal relay race. For each "runner" in the race, give directions to complete simple tasks using ordinals. For example, "First, open your math book. Second, turn to page 100. Third, close your math book."
4. When the first runner completes his task, have him call out "First!" to "tag" his next teammate. Continue with students completing tasks and calling out their positions in the team order to tag following teammates.
5. At the end of the race, present ribbons to the first-, second-, and third-place teams.

## Group 1 ○

**Ordered Chain Links**
1. Give each student a copy of the activity sheet on page 23 and crayons. Ask students to color and cut out each link as directed.
2. Help students staple links together as directed.
3. Ask, "What word is spelled when the chain is finished?" (The chain spells *CORRECT.*) "What order are the colors in?" (The links are ordered red, orange, yellow, green, blue, indigo, violet.)
4. Challenge students to make their own secret words, writing clues to the letter order using ordinal words. Students may wish to write the letters, then write the ordinal number below each letter to help write clues.
5. Ask students to write a reflection in their math notebooks answering the prompt, "How can I show ordinal numbers using words, numbers, and pictures?"

## Group 2 □

**Ordinal Stories**
1. Have students complete the ice cream activity on page 24.
2. Let students color the scoops like their favorite flavors and pretend to order the ice cream using ordinal numbers. For example, "First, I want a scoop of chocolate. Second, I want a scoop of strawberry."
3. Have students complete the caterpillar activity on page 24.
4. Encourage students to write poems or stories about their caterpillars using ordinal numbers. Have students share their ordinal stories or poetry with the group. Each time an ordinal is used, students can clap or snap.
5. Ask students to write a reflection in their math notebooks answering the prompt, "How do I use ordinal numbers to represent or compare position?"

## Group 3 △

**Ordinal Instructions**
1. Have students complete the ordering activity on page 25.
2. Ask students to write the steps using ordinal words. For example, "First, you have a dirty dog. Second, you get a bucket."
3. Challenge students to write directions for different tasks, like making a sandwich or getting dressed, using ordinals.
4. Ask students to share their directions. Let volunteers act out steps as they are read.
5. Ask students to write a reflection in their math notebooks answering the prompt, "How do I use ordinal numbers when giving directions?"

Name_____

Use the labels to color the sections. Cut out each section. Staple
the sections to form a chain of rings in order, first through seventh.
Read the letters on the links to find the secret word.

| 3rd | third | **R** | yellow |
| 7th | seventh | **T** | violet |
| 4th | fourth | **R** | green |
| 1st | first | **C** | red |
| 5th | fifth | **E** | blue |
| 2nd | second | **O** | orange |
| 6th | sixth | **C** | indigo |

cut ✂

Name_____

Color each ice cream scoop. Cut out the scoops. Glue the scoops on the cone in order, 1st through 10th. Color each caterpillar segment. Cut out the segments. Glue the segments to create a caterpillar in order, first through tenth.

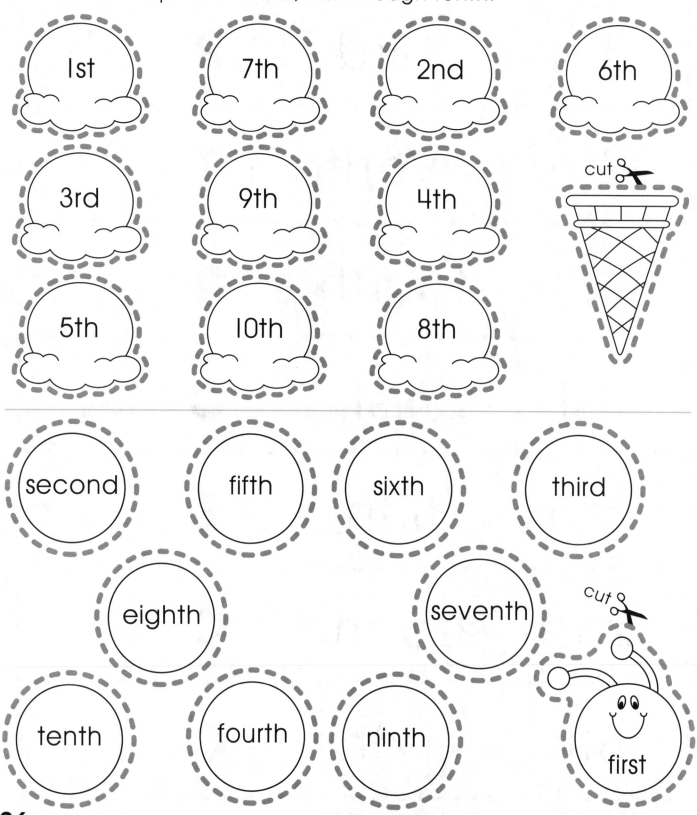

CD-104542 © Carson-Dellosa

Name_____

Each picture shows a step in a story that is out of order. Cut out the pictures. Glue the pictures in the correct order. Write the correct ordinal number under each picture.

cut ✂

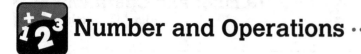

# Number and Operations

**Materials:**
- Coins
- Small prizes
- Paper circle cutouts
- Glue
- Construction paper
- Stapler and staples
- Grocery store advertisement flyers
- Activity sheets (pages 27–29)

## Objective
Understand values of coin combinations.

## Mini-Lesson

1. Give each group of four students a handful of coins.
2. Have students sort the coins. Ask each group how they chose to sort the coins. For example, by color, size, or value.
3. Discuss the value of each coin and model how you can count coin values by skip counting. Have each group count their money.
4. Auction off small prizes. For example, auction a pencil for 8¢. Ask each winning bidder to count the total value of coins aloud. Offer the same prize again, asking for the same value using different coins. Continue to auction prizes until each student wins once. Ensure that each student wins only once and that all coins are collected at the end of the auction.

## Group 1 ○

**Coin Book**
1. Distribute a penny, nickel, dime, and quarter to each student. Distribute half-dollar and dollar coins if desired.
2. Have students examine the coins and draw each on two paper circles (one for the front and one for the back).
3. Have students glue their coin drawings to construction paper pages. Help students label pages with coin names and other information such as values, facts about coin images, and coin metals.
4. Staple the pages together to make coin books.
5. Count aloud five times with each coin value. For example, "1, 2, 3, 4, 5" for pennies and "25, 50, 75, 100, 125" for quarters. Have students write the counting sequences along the bottom of each matching coin page.

## Group 2 □

**What Does Your Name Cost?**
1. Assign each letter of the alphabet a coin:
   Penny: E, A, I, O, U, N, R, T, L, S
   Nickel: D, G, B, C, M, P
   Dime: F, H, V, W, Y
   Quarter: K, J, X, Q, Z
2. Let students calculate the coin values of their first names. Provide coins as manipulatives. Students may want to write their names, choose the coins that match each letter, then add the coins to find the total.
3. Repeat with students' last names. Ask students to compare their first and last name values and volunteer results. Ask, "Can you create the total value of your name with different coins? How much more or less money does your name cost than $1.00?"

## Group 3 △

**Coin Combinations**
1. Provide coins and have students practice making different values with different coins. Ask, "How can you make 75¢ in three different ways? How many pennies are needed to make $1.00? How many dimes?"
2. Let each student browse grocery store advertisement flyers and cut out 3–5 items to purchase. Have students glue grocery items to construction paper.
3. Instruct students to find the necessary coin combination to purchase each item.
4. Have students draw or list the coins they used below each item.
5. Challenge students to find at least two different coin combinations for each grocery item on their papers.

Name_____

Count each set of coins to find the total value. Write the numbers as you count.

1. (1¢) (1¢) (1¢) (1¢) (1¢) (1¢) (1¢) (1¢) = _____ ¢

___ ___ ___ ___ ___ ___ ___ ___

2. (25¢) (25¢) (25¢) (25¢) = _____ ¢ or $_____._____

___ ___ ___ ___

3. (10¢) (10¢) (10¢) (10¢) (10¢) (10¢) (10¢) = _____ ¢

___ ___ ___ ___ ___ ___ ___

4. (5¢) (5¢) (5¢) (5¢) (5¢) (5¢) = _____ ¢

___ ___ ___ ___ ___ ___

5. (5¢) (5¢) (5¢) (5¢) (5¢) (5¢) (5¢) (5¢) = _____ ¢

___ ___ ___ ___ ___ ___ ___ ___

6. (25¢) (25¢) (25¢) (25¢) (25¢) = _____ ¢ or $_____._____

___ ___ ___ ___ ___

Name_____

Find the price of each animal. Write each letter's coin value.
Then, add to find the sum.

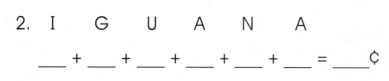

Penny: E, A, I, O, U, N, R, T, L, S          Nickel: D, G, B, C, M, P

Dime: F, H, V, W, Y          Quarter: K, J, X, Q, Z

1. K     I     T     T     E     N

___ + ___ + ___ + ___ + ___ + ___ = ___¢

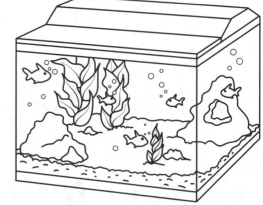

2. I     G     U     A     N     A

___ + ___ + ___ + ___ + ___ + ___ = ___¢

3. T     U     R     T     L     E

___ + ___ + ___ + ___ + ___ + ___ = ___¢

4. H     A     M     S     T     E     R

___ + ___ + ___ + ___ + ___ + ___ + ___ = ___¢

5. P     A     R     A     K     E     E     T

___ + ___ + ___ + ___ + ___ + ___ + ___ + ___ = ___¢

6. G     U     I     N     E     A     P     I     G

___ + ___ + ___ + ___ + ___ + ___ + ___ + ___ + ___ = ___¢

7. C     H     I     N     C     H     I     L     L     A

___ + ___ + ___ + ___ + ___ + ___ + ___ + ___ + ___ + ___ = ___¢

8. Write a word that equals $1.00. _____

**28**

Name_____

Write how many coins you need to buy each item. Then, write a different combination of coins for the same amount.

1.

 76¢

_____ pennies          _____ pennies
_____ nickels          _____ nickels
_____ dimes            _____ dimes
_____ quarters         _____ quarters

2.

 55¢

_____ pennies          _____ pennies
_____ nickels          _____ nickels
_____ dimes            _____ dimes
_____ quarters         _____ quarters

3.

 99¢

_____ pennies          _____ pennies
_____ nickels          _____ nickels
_____ dimes            _____ dimes
_____ quarters         _____ quarters

4.

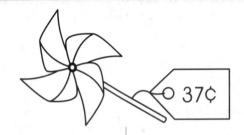 37¢

_____ pennies          _____ pennies
_____ nickels          _____ nickels
_____ dimes            _____ dimes
_____ quarters         _____ quarters

5.

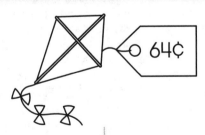 64¢

_____ pennies          _____ pennies
_____ nickels          _____ nickels
_____ dimes            _____ dimes
_____ quarters         _____ quarters

6.

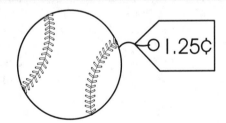 1.25¢

_____ pennies          _____ pennies
_____ nickels          _____ nickels
_____ dimes            _____ dimes
_____ quarters         _____ quarters

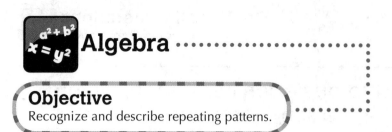

## Algebra

### Objective
Recognize and describe repeating patterns.

**Materials:**
- Pictures of real-world patterns
- Beads
- String
- Rhyming books
- Math notebooks
- Activity sheets (pages 31–33)

### Mini-Lesson

1. Investigate repeating patterns by creating rhythms with the class. Clap, snap, or tap a simple rhythm and have students repeat and continue the pattern.
2. Label the clapping, snapping, and tapping with letters *A*, *B*, and *C*. Then, name the patterns you create. For example, AB is a clap, snap rhythm, and ABC is a clap, snap, tap rhythm.
3. Write several rhythms using letters and ask student volunteers to clap, snap, and tap the patterns.
4. Challenge students to create and label their own rhythm patterns.

### Group 1 ○

**Bead Patterns**
1. Show students pictures of patterns in everyday life such as tiling, wallpaper, and architectural details. Help them describe the patterns they see using letters to name the patterns.
2. Have students create ABAB and ABB bead patterns on string. These patterns can be demonstrated with color, bead shape, bead size, or a combination of features.
3. Ask students to switch patterns with partners. Have students decide which bead should go next in each pattern.
4. Ask students to write a reflection in their math notebooks answering the prompt, "What are some examples of patterns in everyday life?"

### Group 2 ☐

**More Bead Patterns**
1. Have students create AB, ABC, AAB, and ABB bead patterns on string. These patterns can be demonstrated using color, bead size, bead shape, or a combination of features. Each pattern should repeat several times.
2. Ask students to switch patterns with partners. Have them identify the repeated sections and name them using letters.
3. Challenge students to make each pattern on another string with different types of beads. For example, if the given pattern is red, green, red, green (ABAB), the new pattern could be big, small, big, small (ABAB).
4. Ask students to write a reflection in their math notebooks answering the prompt, "How can you describe patterns using letters?"

### Group 3 △

**Translating Poetry**
1. Read favorite rhyming poems or stories and have students identify rhyme patterns.
2. Look at the last word in each line of a poem or story and assign a letter based on the rhyme pattern. For example:
   - AAAA in "Peckin'" or "Alphabalance" by Shel Silverstein
   - ABAB in "Sick" by Shel Silverstein
   - AABB in Dr. Seuss's *Green Eggs and Ham* (Random House, 1960)
   - AABBA in Edwards Lear's *A Book of Nonsense* (Kessinger Publishing, 2010)
3. Have students recreate the rhyme patterns using beads and string or other manipulatives.
4. Encourage students to write rhyming poems using patterns of their own. Have students identify the rhyme patterns using beads and string or other manipulatives.
5. Ask students to write a reflection in their math notebooks answering the prompt "How can you describe rhyme patterns in poetry?"

Name_____

Draw beads on the string to show each pattern. Use colors or shapes to make different beads.

1. ABB ——————————————————

2. AB ——————————————————

3. AAB ——————————————————

Use letters to describe each bead pattern. Draw the bead that should come next.

4. _____

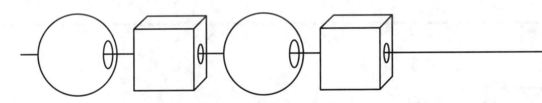

5. _____

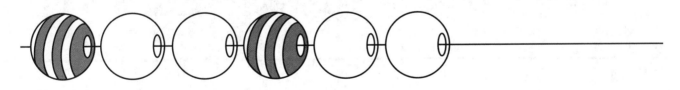

6. _____

Name_____

Draw beads on the string to show each pattern. Use colors or shapes to make different beads.

1. AB _____

2. ABB _____

3. ABC _____

Circle the repeating part of each bead pattern. Use letters to describe the pattern. Draw the same pattern with different beads.

4. _____

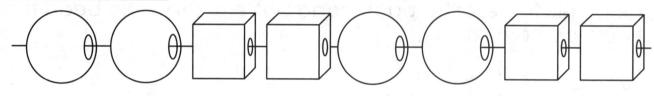

_____

5. _____

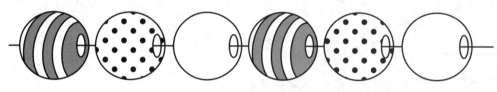

_____

6. _____

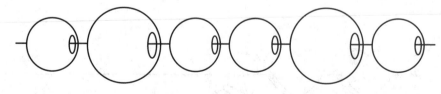

_____

Name_____

Draw each pattern 2 different ways. Use shapes, colors, or pictures.

1. ABC

2. AABC

3. AABBCC

4. ABCB

5. ABCD

6. ABBC

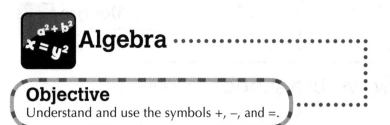 **Algebra**

**Materials:**
- Balance scale
- Counting blocks of equal weight
- Dice
- Index card with "+" printed on one side and "–" on the other
- Math notebooks
- Activity sheets (pages 35–37)

## Objective
Understand and use the symbols +, –, and =.

## Mini-Lesson

1. Use a balance scale to introduce the concept of equality. Place the same number of counting blocks on each side of the balance. Ask, "What makes the pans balanced?" Write an equal sign (=) on the board and point out how it looks like it is balanced.

2. Add blocks to one side of the balance and write an addition sign (+) on the board. Ask, "Do the pans stay balanced when we add blocks to one side? What should we do to keep them balanced?" Students should suggest adding blocks to the other side to maintain balance.

3. Remove the added blocks so that the pans are balanced again. Then, take away blocks from one side and write a subtraction sign (–) on the board. Demonstrate the need to subtract from both sides to keep the pans balanced.

4. Write number sentences on the board and demonstrate them with the scale. Allow student volunteers to attempt demonstration.

    2 + 3 = 5: Place 2 blocks on one side and 5 blocks on the other. Add 3 blocks to balance the scale.

    7 – 3 = 4: Place 7 blocks on one side and 4 blocks on the other. Subtract 3 blocks to balance the scale.

## Group 1 ○

**Plus and Minus**

1. Give each student an index card with an addition sign printed on one side and a subtraction sign printed on the other.

2. Tell simple stories involving addition and subtraction. For example, "Five children are playing at the park when 2 are called home for dinner." Ask students to raise their index cards to show whether each story is an addition or subtraction problem.

3. Using counting blocks on the balance scale, model each story to see what number should be on the other side of the equal sign. Three balances the scale, so 3 children are left at the playground.

4. Repeat with more addition and subtraction stories.

5. Ask students to write a reflection in their math notebooks answering the prompt, "What does '+' mean? What does '–' mean? What does '=' mean?"

## Group 2 □

**Balanced Equations**

1. Place 7 blocks on one side of the scale. Using a die, roll a number and place that many cubes on the other pan.

2. Ask, "How can you balance the scale using addition? Subtraction?" Students should answer that they can add 3 to 4 or subtract 3 from 7.

3. Have students write a number sentence to show each option. Repeat several times with new numbers.

4. Ask students to write a reflection in their math notebooks answering the prompt, "How do you balance a scale when one side is heavier than the other? How does that relate to equations?"

## Group 3 △

**Add or Subtract to Balance**

1. Have students roll two dice and place those numbers of blocks on each side of a balance. For example, if a student rolls 5 and 2, he should place 5 blocks on one side and 2 blocks on the other side.

2. Have students roll one die again and use that as the number to balance both sides to. For example, if a student rolls 4, she must decide whether to add or subtract and by how much on each side so that both sides balance at 4.

3. Have students write number sentences to show their math. For example, 5 – 1 = 2 + 2. Repeat several times with new numbers.

4. Ask students to write a reflection in their math notebooks answering the prompt, "How can you make an equation balanced?"

Name_____

Read each story. Decide if you should use addition or subtraction. Then, draw a picture to solve the problem. Write your answer on the line.

1. Four little monkeys are jumping on the bed. One monkey falls off. How many monkeys are still jumping on the bed?

   _____

2. Three birds are sitting on a telephone wire. Five more birds join them. How many birds are now sitting on the wire?

   _____

3. Three turtles are sunning themselves on a log. One turtle dives into the water. How many turtles are left on the log?

   _____

4. Thirteen cookies are on a cookie sheet. Three children eat 1 cookie each. How many cookies are left on the sheet?

   _____

5. Two chicks are in a nest. Three more chicks hatch in the nest. How many chicks are now in the nest?

   _____

Name_____

Look at each balance scale. Write two number sentences to show how the scale can be balanced.

1.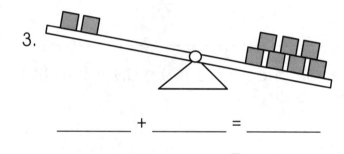

_____ + _____ = _____

_____ − _____ = _____

2.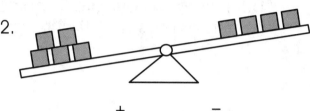

_____ + _____ = _____

_____ − _____ = _____

3.

_____ + _____ = _____

_____ − _____ = _____

4.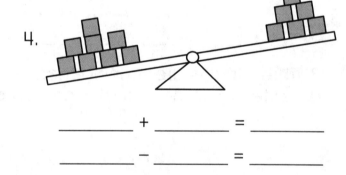

_____ + _____ = _____

_____ − _____ = _____

5.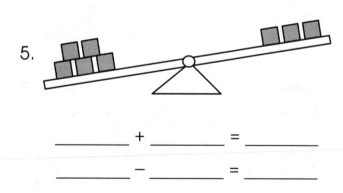

_____ + _____ = _____

_____ − _____ = _____

6.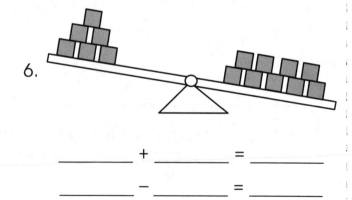

_____ + _____ = _____

_____ − _____ = _____

Name_____

Look at each balance scale. Write number sentences that begin with the numbers on each side. To balance the scale, add the number needed to equal the number given. The first one has been done for you.

1. 10

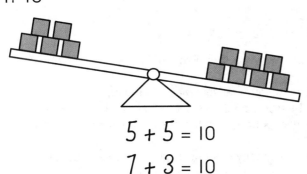

$$5 + 5 = 10$$
$$7 + 3 = 10$$

2. 7

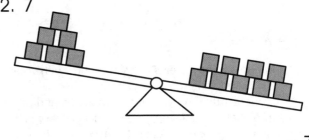

_____ = 7
_____ = 7

3. 5

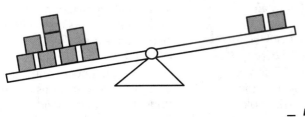

_____ = 5
_____ = 5

4. 3

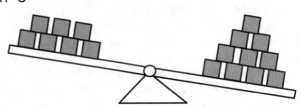

_____ = 3
_____ = 3

5. 9

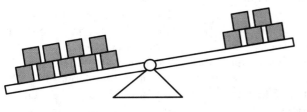

_____ = 9
_____ = 9

6. 6

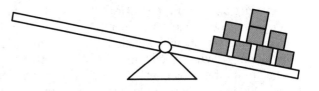

_____ = 6
_____ = 6

 **Algebra** ·······················

## Objective
Create and solve addition and subtraction number sentences.

## Mini-Lesson

1. Configure chairs as seats in a school bus with your chair in the driver's position. Explain that you will act out addition and subtraction sentences.
2. Call out instructions for students to get on and off the bus. Write the number sentences on the board. For example, at the first stop, three students get on: $0 + 3 = 3$. At the next stop, two students get on: $3 + 2 = 5$. At the third stop, one student gets off: $5 - 1 = 4$. Explain that when students get on the bus, you write an addition sentence. When they get off, you write a subtraction sentence.
3. Invite different students to sit in the driver's seat and determine how many passengers get on or off at the next stop. Write the number sentences on the board.

## Group 1 ○

**Number Sentence Stories**
1. Copy the cookie and cookie jar patterns on page 39. Arrange the cookies on top of the jar as you count the total with students.
2. Using each student's name, sing, "Who took the cookies from the cookie jar? [Student name] took the cookies from the cookie jar. Who, me? Yes, you. Not me! Then, who?"
3. Each time a student's name is sung, let him take a certain number of cookies from the jar and set them aside.
4. After a student takes cookies, ask the group to tell a number story and sentence that matches what happened. For example, "Sarah had 10 cookies. She took 4 cookies away. Now, 6 cookies are in the cookie jar: $10 - 4 = 6$."
5. Repeat the activity with addition by singing, "Who baked the cookies for the cookie jar?"
6. Ask students to write a reflection in their math notebooks answering the prompt, "What is a number sentence?"

## Group 2 ▢

**Writing Number Sentences**
1. Copy the cookie and cookie jar patterns on page 39 for pairs of students.
2. Sing "Who Took the Cookies from the Cookie Jar?" Give each pair of students 15 cookie cutouts and a cookie jar cutout. Help students tape their cookie jar patterns to paper bags to create cookie "jars."
3. Have students start with all of the cookies inside the cookie jars. Tell students to take some cookies out and write that number on the plate on the activity sheet (page 40). Then, have pairs of students determine how many cookies are left inside their jars without looking inside.
4. Have students complete the number sentence and count the remaining cookies to check their answers.
5. Ask students to write a reflection in their math notebooks answering the prompt, "How can you tell a number story based on one of the number sentences you wrote in the activity?"

## Group 3 △

**Multistep Problems**
1. Follow steps 1–3 of the Group 1 lesson, calling two or more students in succession to either take or bake cookies.
2. Write the starting number of cookies on the board and keep track of students' actions as each student takes away or adds to the cookie jar. For example, write $5 + 4 - 3$ to show students started with 5 cookies, baked 4 cookies, and took 3 cookies.
3. Have students solve the problem and count the cookies to check their answers. Ask, "What number did you add or subtract first? Does the order you add or subtract matter?"
4. Have students write multistep story problems and switch with partners to solve.
5. Ask students to write a reflection in their math notebooks answering the prompt, "What do you do when solving multistep problems?"

Name_____

Use the cookies and cookie jar patterns with the lessons on page 38.

Name_____

Use cookies to write addition and subtraction sentences. For each sentence, write the number of cookies you start with in the first jar. Write + or – in the square. Write the number of cookies eaten (subtracted) or baked (added) on the plate. Add or subtract. Write the final number of cookies in the last jar.

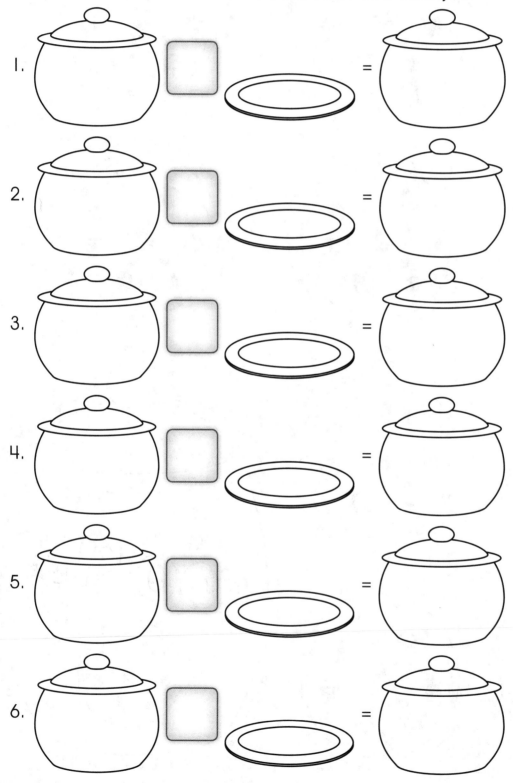

Name_____

## Write and solve a number sentence for each story.

1. A cookie jar has 10 cookies in it. Henry takes 3 cookies. Brianna places 6 more in the jar. How many cookies are in the jar now?

_____

2. A cookie jar has 8 cookies in it. Pedro places 4 more in the jar. Nina takes 5 cookies. Maria takes 2 cookies. How many cookies are in the jar now?

_____

3. A cookie jar has 15 cookies in it. Grace takes 9 cookies. Ian takes 3 cookies. Victor places 7 more in the jar. Patty places 5 more in the jar. How many cookies are in the jar now?

_____

4. A cookie jar has 12 cookies in it. Rachael places 8 more in the jar. Dylan takes 5 cookies. Lisa places 2 more in the jar. Jake takes 10 cookies. How many cookies are in the jar now?

_____

5. A cookie jar has some cookies in it. Nathan places 4 more in the jar. Cara takes 7 cookies. Wendy takes 2 cookies. Leon places 9 more in the jar. Now, 13 cookies are in the jar. How many cookies were in the jar to begin with?

_____

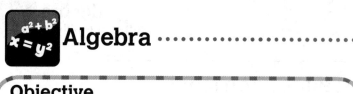

# Algebra

## Objective

Understand addition and subtraction as inverse operations.

**Materials:**
- Play money
- Two-color counters
- Red and blue crayons
- Math notebooks
- Activity sheets (pages 43–45)

## Mini-Lesson

1. Play an inverse operations banking game. Play a banker and distribute $10 to each student. Ask, "How much money did you start with? How much was added? How much do you have now?" Write $0 + 10 = 10$ on the board to demonstrate writing a matching number sentence.
2. Now, ask each student to pay a $10 fee to the bank. Ask, "How much money did you start with? How much was taken away? How much do you have now?" Write $10 - 10 = 0$ on the board and demonstrate the inverse equation.
3. Repeat with different monetary amounts. Ask students to write number sentences describing the transactions.
4. Discuss the inverse nature of addition and subtraction as students end with the same amount of money they started with. Explain that subtracting "undoes" adding and adding undoes subtracting.

## Group 1 ○

### Modeling Math Facts

1. Give each student 5 two-color counters. Ask them to flip the counters so that 3 are one color and 2 are the other color.
2. Ask, "What math fact can you write for this model?" Write all student responses. Students will likely see the model in different ways and offer different addition and subtraction facts. For example, $3 + 2 = 5$ or $2 + 3 = 5$.
3. Have students separate one color set from the other color set. Ask, "What math fact can you write for this action?" Write all student responses. For example, $5 - 2 = 3$ or $5 - 3 = 2$.
4. Ask, "How many different facts did we write? How many numbers did we use to make all four facts?"
5. Let students explore more facts with different numbers of counters.
6. Ask students to write a reflection in their math notebooks answering the prompt, "How are addition and subtraction related?"

## Group 2 ☐

### Fact Family Houses

1. Draw a house using a square and a triangle. Write two numbers in the bottom corners of the roof. Show the numbers with two-color counters. Write the sum of the numbers at the top of the roof.
2. Ask, "What addition fact can we write with these numbers? How else can we write the same fact?" Let students flip the counters to switch the operands. Ask, "Does changing the numbers' order change the sum?" Write the two addition facts inside the house.
3. Ask, "How can we write a subtraction fact using these same numbers?" Let students switch the counters again, taking away one color of counters and then the other. Write the two subtraction facts below the addition facts.
4. Explain that the three numbers create a fact family of related addition and subtraction facts.
5. Ask students to write a reflection in their math notebooks answering the prompt, "What is a fact family?"

## Group 3 △

### Missing Numbers

1. Draw three triangles on the board. Label the top corner and one lower corner of each with two of the three numbers for a fact family.
2. Have students determine the missing operand and write the related facts for each triangle. Ask, "Did you use addition or subtraction to find the missing number? What would happen if you used addition to find it?"
3. After several missing operand examples, show students triangles with just the top number given. Ask, "How can you find the missing numbers? Will everyone write the same facts? Why or why not?"
4. Ask students to write a reflection in their math notebooks answering the prompt, "Can fact families have less than four facts? Explain."

Name_____

Find all of the fact families for 10 using the trains as a guide. The first train shows the fact family for 10 + 0 = 10. Color all of the cars red. The next train shows 9 + 1 = 10. Color 9 cars red and 1 car blue. Write numbers on the lines to complete the fact family. Continue the pattern to color and write all of the fact families for 10.

1.

10 + 0 = 10

0 + 10 = 10

10 – 0 = 10

10 – 10 = 0

2.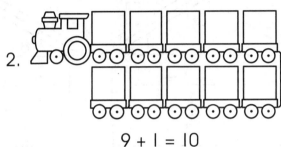

9 + 1 = 10

_____ + _____ = _____

_____ – _____ = _____

_____ – _____ = _____

3.

8 + 2 = 10

_____ + _____ = _____

_____ – _____ = _____

_____ – _____ = _____

4.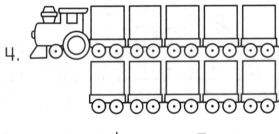

_____ + _____ = _____

_____ + _____ = _____

_____ – _____ = _____

_____ – _____ = _____

5.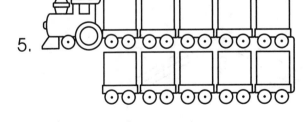

_____ + _____ = _____

_____ + _____ = _____

_____ – _____ = _____

_____ – _____ = _____

6.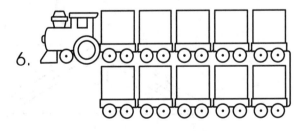

_____ + _____ = _____

_____ – _____ = _____

Name_____

Use the numbers on each roof to create a fact family. Write the numbers on the lines to complete each number sentence. Write any missing roof numbers.

1.
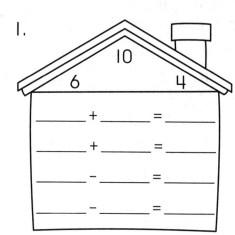

10
6      4

____ + ____ = ____
____ + ____ = ____
____ − ____ = ____
____ − ____ = ____

2.
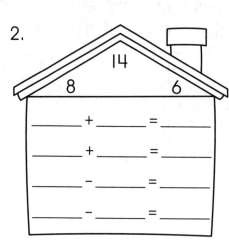

14
8      6

____ + ____ = ____
____ + ____ = ____
____ − ____ = ____
____ − ____ = ____

3.
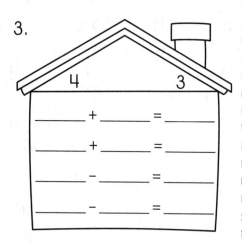

4      3

____ + ____ = ____
____ + ____ = ____
____ − ____ = ____
____ − ____ = ____

4.
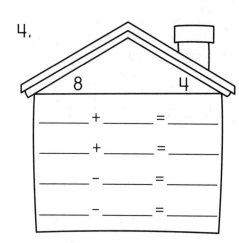

8      4

____ + ____ = ____
____ + ____ = ____
____ − ____ = ____
____ − ____ = ____

5.
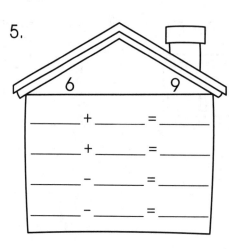

6      9

____ + ____ = ____
____ + ____ = ____
____ − ____ = ____
____ − ____ = ____

6.
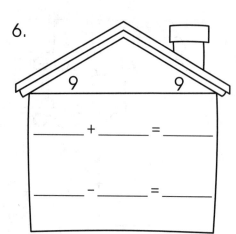

9      9

____ + ____ = ____

____ − ____ = ____

7.
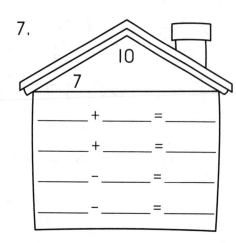

10
7

____ + ____ = ____
____ + ____ = ____
____ − ____ = ____
____ − ____ = ____

8.

8
5

____ + ____ = ____
____ + ____ = ____
____ − ____ = ____
____ − ____ = ____

**44**

Name_____

Use the numbers provided to write fact families. Find the missing numbers.

1.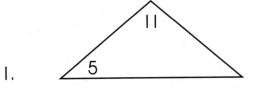

_____ + _____ = _____

_____ + _____ = _____

_____ − _____ = _____

_____ − _____ = _____

2.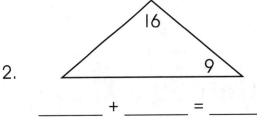

_____ + _____ = _____

_____ + _____ = _____

_____ − _____ = _____

_____ − _____ = _____

3.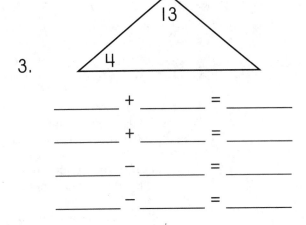

_____ + _____ = _____

_____ + _____ = _____

_____ − _____ = _____

_____ − _____ = _____

4.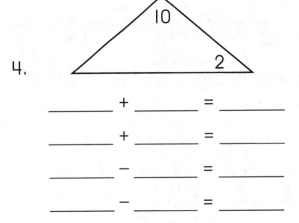

_____ + _____ = _____

_____ + _____ = _____

_____ − _____ = _____

_____ − _____ = _____

Write your own fact families.

5.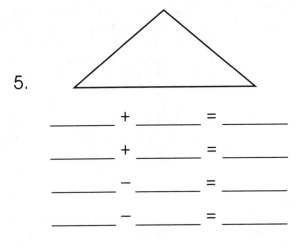

_____ + _____ = _____

_____ + _____ = _____

_____ − _____ = _____

_____ − _____ = _____

6.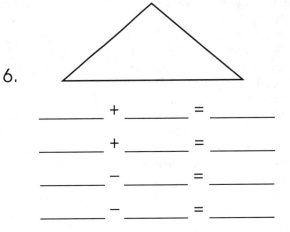

_____ + _____ = _____

_____ + _____ = _____

_____ − _____ = _____

_____ − _____ = _____

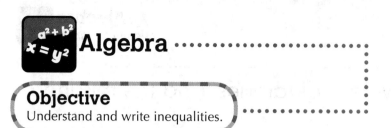

# Algebra

## Objective
Understand and write inequalities.

**Materials:**
- Index cards marked with > or <
- Index cards marked with random numbers from 1–100
- Music player
- Math notebooks
- Sets of number cards 0–9
- Activity sheets (pages 47–49)

## Mini-Lesson

1. Show students cards with > and < signs. Explain what each symbol means.
2. Have two students each choose a number card and stand at the front of the class. Stand between the students and hold the > and < signs. Ask students which symbol is correct.
3. Model for students how to read the inequality. For example, *85 > 49* is read, "Eighty-five is greater than forty-nine."
4. Have the students with numbers change positions and ask if the symbol also needs to change.
5. Play "Musical Inequalities." Post several > and < cards around the room. Give each student a random number card. Play music. When the music stops, have students form pairs near the closest inequality symbol and stand on either side of the symbol to make a true inequality.

## Group 1 ○

**Hungry Alligator**
1. Teach students an easy way to remember which inequality sign to use. Hold your arms out to one side and pretend to be a hungry alligator. Tell students that the alligator wants to eat the bigger number. Show students how the inequality signs look like the hungry alligator's mouth.
2. Invite three students to demonstrate. One student should stand in the middle as the alligator, and the other two each choose a number card. Ask the alligator to look at the numbers and open his "mouth" toward the bigger number.
3. Have the rest of the group read the inequality aloud, using the words *greater than* or *less than*. Repeat with different numbers and students.
4. Ask students to write a reflection in their math notebooks answering the prompt, "How can you use symbols to compare numbers?"

## Group 2 □

**Making Inequalities**
1. Arrange students in pairs. Give each pair a stack of 20 number cards and five of each inequality symbol card.
2. Have students order their cards in side-by-side columns, top to bottom from least to greatest.
3. Have students work together to choose the correct symbol to compare each pair of side-by-side numbers. Challenge students to find who has more greater numbers.
4. Have each student with more lesser numbers reorder his numbers top to bottom from greatest to least and compare again. Does it change the outcome of the game? Have students choose new numbers and play again.
5. Ask students to write a reflection in their math notebooks answering the prompt, "What does *greater than* mean? How can you change an inequality from 'less than' to 'greater than'?"

## Group 3 △

**Place-Value Game**
1. Have each student divide a sheet of paper in half and label the left side *tens* and the right side *ones*. (Some students may want to divide their papers in thirds and add *hundreds* for an extra challenge.) Provide each student with a facedown set of number cards 0–9.
2. Arrange students in pairs to play. The first player turns over a number card and decides where to put it on her place value chart with the object of creating the greatest number. Once she places the card, she cannot remove it.
3. The next player turns over a number card and decides where to put it on his chart. Repeat so that each player makes a two-digit number.
4. The player with the greater number wins the round. Students should record rounds by writing both two-digit numbers in their math notebooks and comparing the numbers with a > or < sign. Play as many rounds as desired.

Name_____

Write the correct symbol, > or <, between each number pair.

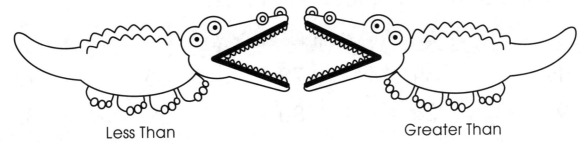

Less Than                                        Greater Than

1. 56 _____ 65            2. 45 _____ 98

3. 12 _____ 40            4. 88 _____ 66

5. 36 _____ 33            6. 29 _____ 92

7. 77 _____ 71            8. 64 _____ 69

Write your own inequalities.

9. _____ > _____

10. _____ < _____

Choose numbers from the number bank to complete the inequalities. Use each number only once.

| Number Bank | | | | |
|---|---|---|---|---|
| 49 | 64 | 72 | 55 | 17 |
| 91 | 26 | 80 | 39 | 33 |

1. 83 < _____

2. _____ < 22

3. 31 > _____

4. _____ > 75

5. _____ > 68

6. 40 > _____

7. 48 < _____

8. _____ < 61

9. 13 < _____

10. _____ > 57

Name_____

Write the digits in the tens or ones columns to complete true inequalities.

| | Tens | Ones | | Tens | Ones |
|---|---|---|---|---|---|
| 1. 4, 6, 1, 0 | ___ | ___ | > | ___ | ___ |
| 2. 3, 2, 9, 5 | ___ | ___ | > | ___ | ___ |
| 3. 3, 8, 1 | 8 | ___ | < | ___ | ___ |
| 4. 7, 0, 0, 4 | ___ | ___ | > | ___ | ___ |
| 5. 5, 2, 9, 3 | ___ | ___ | < | ___ | ___ |
| 6. 7, 4 | 5 | ___ | > | ___ | 8 |
| 7. 6, 5, 0 | ___ | 9 | < | ___ | ___ |
| 8. 1, 8 | ___ | 2 | > | 7 | ___ |

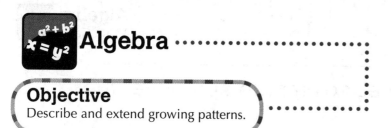

# Algebra

**Materials:**
- Geometric shapes building blocks
- Dry spaghetti broken into short lengths
- O-shaped cereal
- Math notebooks
- Activity sheets (pages 51–53)

## Mini-Lesson

1. Introduce linear growing patterns using geometric shapes building blocks. Display 1 block, then 2 stacked blocks, 3 stacked blocks, and 4 stacked blocks. In this linear pattern, each stack is one taller than the previous.
2. Ask, "Can you describe this pattern? What would the next stack look like? What rule could you write to help make the next stack? How many blocks would be in the 100th stack?"
3. Show another pattern: 1 square with 2 triangles stacked on its right side, 1 square with 4 stacked triangles, 1 square with 6 stacked triangles. Ask students to use blocks to build the next step in the pattern. Ask, "What is the pattern rule? How many triangles would be stacked in the 20th figure?"
4. Encourage students to use blocks to build the first three steps of their own growing patterns and challenge partners to build the fourth.

## Group 1 ○

**Extending Patterns**
1. Give each student a handful of spaghetti and a copy of the activity sheet on page 51.
2. Instruct students to complete the activity sheet by gluing short spaghetti pieces to the pictures to extend each pattern. Students may also wish to glue pasta over the existing pattern lines.
3. Ask students to describe each pattern. Ask "How did you predict the next step? How are the patterns different? The same?"
4. After completing the activity sheet, let students use the pasta to create their own growing patterns. Challenge the group to make the next steps.
5. Ask students to write a reflection in their math notebooks answering the prompt, "What is a growing pattern?"

## Group 2 □

**Pattern Rules**
1. Give each student a handful of o-shaped cereal and a copy of the activity sheet on page 52.
2. Instruct students to complete the activity sheet by gluing the o-shaped cereal to the pictures to extend each pattern.
3. Ask students to describe each pattern. Ask, "What was the rule for each pattern? How could you tell? How many cereal pieces would you need for the 10th train? Do any patterns have an end point? Why or why not?"
4. Encourage students to use the o-shaped cereal to create their own growing patterns that increase or decrease. Have students share and compare their patterns, and switch with partners to write a rule for each pattern.
5. Ask students to write a reflection in their math notebooks answering the prompt, "How are growing patterns different from repeating patterns? How are they the same?"

## Group 3 △

**Functions**
1. Provide each student with a copy of the activity sheet on page 53.
2. The engines on the activity sheet show pattern rules, and the first car of each train gives the beginning number. Have students apply each rule to complete the pattern on the remaining cars.
3. After completing the activity, have students number the train cars 1–10 (not including the engine) and encourage them to notice a relationship between the car number and the pattern number inside the car. Challenge students to determine the 20th, 50th, and 100th numbers for each pattern.
4. Ask students to write a reflection in their math notebooks answering the prompt, "How can you describe a particular growing pattern using numbers and math symbols?"

Name_____

## Glue spaghetti to continue the patterns.

1.

2.

3.

Glue o-shaped cereal as puffs of steam to continue the patterns.
Then, describe each pattern rule.

I.

_____

2.

_____

3.

_____

Name_____

Use the rule on each train engine to complete the pattern on the train cars. Write any missing rules.

1.

2.

3.

4.

5.

6.

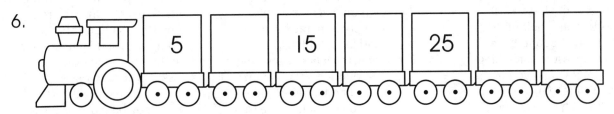

Write your own rule and pattern.

7.

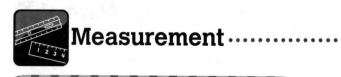

# Measurement

## Objective
Measure and compare using nonstandard units.

**Materials:**
- Several different lengths of string
- Wooden craft sticks
- 2"-wide cardboard strips
- 2"-wide colorful paper strips
- Scissors
- Glue
- 1/2" square graph paper
- Linking cubes
- Paper clips (small and large)
- Math notebooks
- Activity sheets (pages 55–57)

## Mini-Lesson

1. Show students a length of string and challenge them to find an object in the classroom that is the same length, longer, and shorter.
2. Ask students to share their answers. Let several students use the string to measure and compare the objects they found to see if their estimates are correct.
3. Ask, "How can you use the string to measure something longer than the string? Shorter?" Choose objects from around the room and ask how many string lengths they are.
4. Show several different lengths of string. Ask, "If we lay 10 of these strings along the chalkboard edge, can we say that the chalkboard is 10 strings long? Why or why not?"
5. Explain to students that in nonstandard measurement, the unit length cannot change while measuring.

## Group 1 ○

**Using a Nonstandard Unit to Measure**

1. Give each student a wooden craft stick to measure with. Show students how to align the end of a stick with the end of an object to measure.
2. Let students search the classroom for things that are shorter than, longer than, or the same length as their craft sticks.
3. Ask students to identify things that are 1 stick long, 2 sticks long, and 3 sticks long.
4. At the end of the lesson, ask students to share their findings. Ask, "Did you need to have 3 sticks to measure something 3 sticks long? Could you use your craft stick to measure a paper clip? Why or why not?"
5. Ask students to write a reflection in their math notebooks answering the prompt, "How can you compare the lengths of different objects?"

## Group 2 ☐

**Make Your Own Ruler**

1. Have students make their own rulers with 2"-wide strips of cardboard and colorful squares of paper.
2. Help each student stack 6 different colorful paper strips and cut off a desired length to make units of the same length. Have students glue their 6 units end-to-end onto a strip of cardboard.
3. Let students number each unit from left to right and name their own units. For example, a student could name his units *blops* and label 6 blops.
4. Let students practice measuring objects around the classroom. Ask, "If you and a friend each used your own rulers to measure the same book, would you get the same results? Would it be useful to tell a salesperson the size of a picture frame you need in *blops*? Why or why not?"
5. Ask students to write a reflection in their math notebooks answering the prompt, "How are objects measured?"

## Group 3 △

**Scale Maps**

1. Discuss scale drawings and show examples of maps. Have students use steps as a nonstandard measure to create a scale drawing of the classroom.
2. Show students how to step heel-to-toe to make sure their steps are even as they walk the length and the width of the room. Have them measure classroom furniture in the same manner.
3. Use the measurements to draw scale maps of the classroom on graph paper. One square equals one step. Students should label their maps and include a scale at the bottom of the maps.
4. Ask, "Will everyone's measurements be the same? Will they be close or vastly different? Why? If you measured the furniture with your hands instead of your feet, could you show them both on your scale drawing as equaling 1 square?"
5. Ask students to write a reflection in their math notebooks answering the prompt, "What is a nonstandard unit of measure?"

Name_____

Find objects around the room to follow the directions. Write each object name on the line.

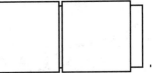

1. _____ is shorter than _____ .

2. _____ is the same length as

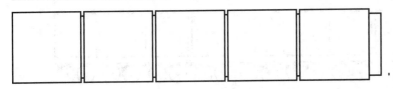

3. _____ is longer than

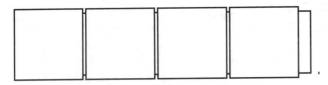

4. _____ is longer than

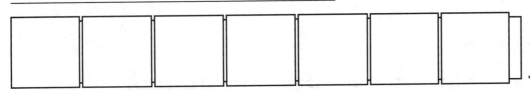

5. _____ is the same length as

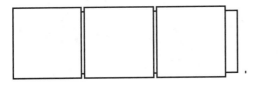

6. _____ is shorter than

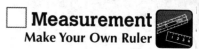
Name_____

Use linking cubes to measure each object. Write how many cubes long each object is.

1.

_____ cubes

2.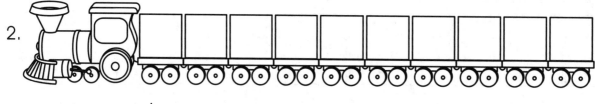

_____ cubes

3.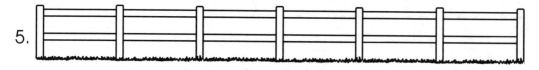

_____ cubes

4.

_____ cubes

5.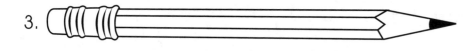

_____ cubes

Name_____

Use small and large paper clips to measure each object. Round to the nearest whole paper clip. Write how many small and large paper clips long each object is.

1.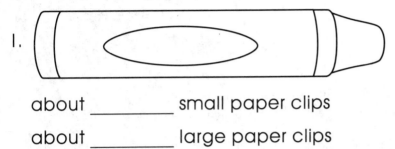

about _____ small paper clips

about _____ large paper clips

2.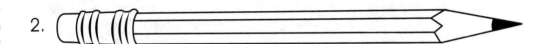

about _____ small paper clips

about _____ large paper clips

3.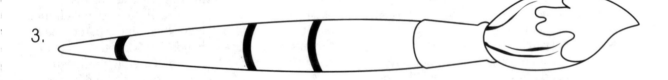

about _____ small paper clips

about _____ large paper clips

Use your measurements to answer the questions.

4. Did you use more or fewer small paper clips than large paper clips to measure each object? Why?

_____

5. Are paper clips a good measuring tool? Why or why not?

_____

 **Measurement**

## Objective
Choose and compare appropriate standard measurements.

**Materials:**
- Collection of classroom objects
- Collection of measuring tools
- Index cards
- Masking tape
- Math notebooks
- Activity sheets (pages 59–61)

## Mini-Lesson

1. Display different objects at the front of the class. Show tall, short, heavy, and light objects.
2. Ask students to describe the objects in terms of their size and compare them to each other. Write the statements on the board.
3. Ask, "How can we describe the size of the objects in a more specific way?" Have students brainstorm a list of standard measurements (inch, centimeter, pound, gram, etc.).
4. Challenge students to match their general descriptions of the objects with the appropriate standard measuring units that could be used to describe the objects instead. For example, *the book is heavy* could match the standard measuring units of pounds or kilograms.
5. Ask, "Would we use kilometers to measure a paper clip? Why not? Which standard measurements are best for small objects and which are best for large objects?"

## Group 1 ◯

**Measurement Tools**

1. Provide a variety of measuring tools for students to examine.
2. Make several sets of matching index cards printed with names of measuring tools and units of measure. For example, a balance scale card and a gram or ounce card, a bathroom scale card and a pound or kilogram card, a ruler card and an inch or centimeter card, a yard/meter stick card and a foot/yard or meter card, and a thermometer card and a degrees Fahrenheit or Celsius card.
3. Let pairs of students play a matching memory game.
4. Ask students to write a reflection in their math notebooks answering the prompt, "Why are there different tools for different units of measurement?"

## Group 2 ▢

**Comparing Measurements**

1. Explain to students that some units of measurement are best for measuring large things, and some are best for measuring small things.
2. Write units of measurement on index cards. Make a set of standard-length unit cards and a set of metric-length unit cards.
3. Divide a table in half with masking tape and label one half *large* and one half *small*. Have students place each unit card under the correct heading.
4. Let students order each set (standard and metric) from smallest to largest unit. Ask, "Which metric unit would you use to measure the height of a tree? Which measurement makes more sense for the length of a room: 15 inches or 15 feet?"
5. Ask students to write a reflection in their math notebooks answering the prompt, "Why do we need different units of measurement?"

## Group 3 △

**Estimating Measurements**

1. Give each student an inch ruler. Have them find a part of their hands that is about 1 inch long (width of a thumb or length of a section of finger) and a part of their arms that is about 1 foot long (length of a forearm with or without hand).
2. Explain that it can be useful when you do not have a ruler handy to have a reference for estimating lengths. You may wish to have students choose a referent for centimeters as well.
3. Provide students with several classroom objects to measure using their estimation referents.
4. Ask, "About how long is my desk? Which object is about 8 feet long?" After students have made their estimates, help them check their measurements using standard measurement tools.
5. Ask students to write a reflection in their math notebooks answering the prompt, "When might you need to estimate measurements?"

Name_____

# Circle the best tool for measuring.

1.

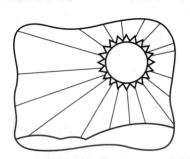

2.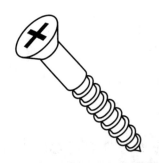

3.

4.

5. meters

6. pounds

7. grams

8. inches

Name_____

## Circle the smaller measurement.

1. 3 centimeters      3 kilometers

2. 6 yards      6 feet

3. 20 ounces      20 pounds

4. 1 meter      1 millimeter

## Circle the best measurement.

5.       450 kilograms      450 grams

6.       10 feet      10 inches

7.       7 meters      7 centimeters

8. 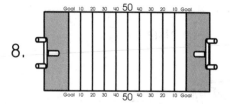      100 yards      100 miles

**60**

Name_____

Use two fingertips, side by side, to estimate the length of each object in inches. Then, use a ruler to measure the actual length in inches.

1.

Estimate: _____ inches

Actual: _____ inches

2.

Estimate: _____ inches

Actual: _____ inches

3.

Estimate: _____ inches

Actual: _____ inch

4.

Estimate: _____ inches

Actual: _____ inches

5.

Estimate: _____ inches

Actual: _____ inches

# Measurement

**Materials:**
- Small white paper plates
- Brass paper fasteners
- Construction paper
- Small whiteboards
- Write-on/wipe-away markers
- Demonstration clocks (digital and analog)
- Math notebooks
- Activity sheets (pages 63–65)

## Objective

Tell time to the nearest half hour and relate time to daily activities.

## Mini-Lesson

1. Complete a KWL chart about telling time. Ask students what they already know, what they want to know, and (later in the lesson) what they have learned.
2. Distribute paper plates. Help each student create a clock by attaching construction paper hands with a brass paper fastener. Have students identify the hour and minute hands on their clocks. Ask, "How many hours are on the clock? What happens after the 12th hour?"
3. Call out times to the half hour for students to show on their clocks.
4. Write digital times on the board to match the times students show on their analog clocks. Ask, "How are digital and analog clocks the same? How are they different?"
5. To close the lesson, complete the last column in the KWL chart.

## Group 1 ○

**Examining Half Hours**

1. Show an analog clock and a digital clock both set to 4:30. Have students identify the part of each clock that tells the hour and the part that tells the minute. Ask, "What time is this? What is another way to say this time?"
2. Ask students how many minutes are in 1 hour. Have students look at the analog clock as a circle divided in half by the hands. Ask, "Why is this time said to be 'half past'? How many minutes are in half of an hour?
3. Ask, "Can you tell from the hour part of the digital clock that this is a half-hour time? Can you tell from the hour hand of the analog clock? How?"
4. Let students use their paper clocks from the mini-lesson and write-on/wipe-away markers to practice writing half-hour times.
5. Ask students to write a reflection in their math notebooks answering the prompt, "Which type of clock do you prefer? Why?"

## Group 2 □

**Times Throughout the Day**

1. Engage students in a discussion about what they do at different times of the day. Ask, "What do you do every day? Around what time do you (wake up, eat lunch, go to bed)? How can you know about what time of day it is without looking at a clock?"
2. Have students draw pictures to show at least five things they do at certain times every day. For example, a student might draw herself waking up, playing at recess, watching TV, eating dinner, and going to bed.
3. Have students write a digital time beside each picture and draw an analog clock showing that time.
4. Let students share their pictures and practice reading times from each other's pictures.
5. Ask students to write a reflection in their math notebooks answering the prompt, "What are different ways to tell when it's time to do certain things throughout the day?"

## Group 3 △

**School Schedules**

1. Ask students to create a class schedule for one school day. Beginning with the first bell, list each activity (reading, math, lunch, etc.) throughout the day. Students can list activities as regularly scheduled, or they can create a list of new activities and subjects they wish the school day consisted of.
2. Beside each scheduled activity, have students write the time. Remind students to write A.M. and P.M. to denote activities that happen before noon and after noon.
3. Let students share their schedules and have the group use their paper clocks to show the times. Ask, "Can you show A.M. and P.M. on an analog clock? Would it make sense for lunch to be at 12:30 A.M.?"
4. Ask students to write a reflection in their math notebooks answering the prompt, "If 24 hours are in a day, why do we use 12-hour clocks?"

Name_____

## Draw hands on each clock to show the time given.

1.

six thirty or half past six

2.

eleven o'clock

3.

seven o'clock

4.

eight thirty or half past eight

## Use words to write the time that is shown on each clock.

5.

_____

6.

_____

7.

_____

8.

_____

Name_____

Draw a line to match each activity to the clock that shows the best time for that activity.

1.

2.

3.

4.

Draw hands on each clock to show the best time for that activity.

5.

6.

7.

8.

**64**

Name_____

Write the numbers 1 to 10 to put the zookeeper's schedule in order. Then, write the correct time from the time bank next to each activity in the schedule.

| Time Bank | | | | |
|---|---|---|---|---|
| 10:00 A.M. | 4:30 P.M. | 3:00 P.M. | 7:00 A.M. | 6:30 P.M. |
| 8:00 A.M. | 12:30 P.M. | 8:30 A.M. | 7:30 A.M. | 10:00 P.M. |

_____  arrive at zoo                                    _____

_____  eat lunch                                        _____

_____  dinner for animals                               _____

_____  wake up                                          _____

_____  lead a mid-morning tour                          _____

_____  eat breakfast                                    _____

_____  breakfast for animals                            _____

_____  go to bed                                        _____

_____  eat dinner                                       _____

_____  clean habitats before closing                    _____

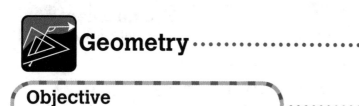

# Geometry

**Materials:**
- Towels and sheets
- Cardboard boxes
- Paper
- Crayons
- Stapler and staples
- Map of the United States
- Maps of tourist attractions (zoo, amusement park, etc.)
- Math notebooks
- Activity sheets (pages 67–69)

## Mini-Lesson

1. Create an obstacle course that students can go over, under, around, between, and through. Obstacles might include a "river" (towel or sheet) to jump over, a table to go around or under, rows of chairs to go between, and a cardboard box tunnel to go through.
2. Describe to students how they are to move through the course using positional vocabulary: over, around, below, under, between, above, up, down, behind, in front of, next to, left or right of, etc.
3. Afterward, invite students to describe the course. Each time they use a positional word, write it on the board.

## Group 1 ◯

**Positional Vocabulary**
1. Brainstorm with students a vocabulary list of positional words.
2. Play Simon Says using these words. For example, "Simon says, duck *below* the table. Simon says, stand *in front of* your chair."
3. After the game, have students use paper and crayons to illustrate a picture book showing one positional word per page. Students can draw pictures from the game or something simple like a star under a box.
4. Students should write a caption for each page using a positional word to describe the picture. Staple the pages together to finish the book.
5. Ask students to write a reflection in their math notebooks answering the prompt, "How can you describe where something is?"

## Group 2 ▢

**Positions on a Map**
1. Look at a map of the United States (or another country). Ask questions like, "What state is below Kansas? North Carolina is to the right of what state?"
2. Have each student draw a 3 x 3 grid and draw a simple symbol or letter in each square.
3. Have students give directions to a partner telling how to fill in a blank 3 x 3 grid to look like theirs without showing the completed grid.
4. Ask students to write a reflection in their math notebooks answering the prompt, "What words can you use to describe where something is?"

## Group 3 △

**20 Positional Questions**
1. Using maps of a zoo, an amusement park, or another tourist attraction, have pairs of students play 20 Questions.
2. Have one student choose a secret destination on the map. Her partner will ask yes or no questions to guess the destination. For example, one could ask, "Is it next to the Ferris wheel?" or "Is it above the train station?" Once the destination is correctly guessed, have students switch and play again.
3. Challenge students to give positional information to partners about a room in their homes while the partners draw maps based on the directions given.
4. Let partners switch maps to check their directing and drawing accuracy.
5. Ask students to write a reflection in their math notebooks answering the prompt, "What is the difference between position and direction?"

CD-104542 © Carson-Dellosa

Name_____

Write words to describe the locations of the objects.

1. The player throws the basketball _____ her head.

2. The plane flies _____ the clouds.

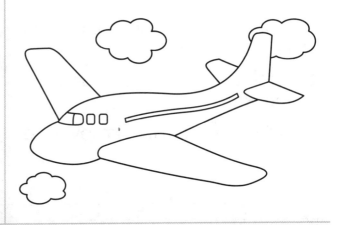

3. The fish swim _____ the shark.

4. The tree is _____ the house.

5. The child is _____ the book.

6. The horse is _____ the cart.

Name_____

Follow the directions to complete the grid.

1. Draw a heart above the star.

2. Draw a triangle to the left of the heart.

3. Write *H* next to the star but not under the triangle.

4. Draw a circle under the *H*.

5. Write *8* near the heart and the *H*.

6. Draw a smiley face beside the star.

7. Write *W* below the smiley face.

8. Draw a rectangle between the *W* and circle.

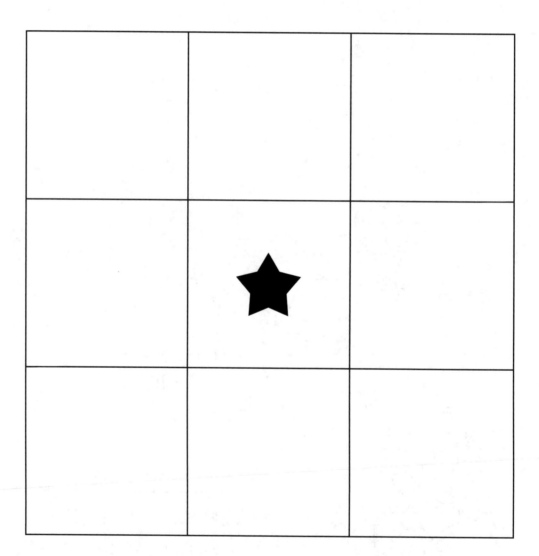

Name_____

Use the map to locate the attractions at the amusement park. Use the words *near*, *far*, *behind*, *in front of*, *between*, *next to*, *left of*, and *right of*.

1. The Ferris wheel is _____.

2. The roller coaster is _____.

3. The cotton candy stand is _____.

4. The water slide is _____.

5. The balloon vendor is _____.

6. The ice cream cart is _____.

7. The bouncy castle is _____.

8. The ticket booth is _____.

 **Geometry** ·············

## Objective

Recognize and draw triangles, rectangles, squares, and circles.

### Materials:

- Index cards
- Tape
- 11" x 18" paper
- Geometric shape blocks (building, pattern, or tangram)
- Scissors
- Construction paper
- Toy hoops
- Activity sheets (pages 71–73)

## Mini-Lesson

1. Write clues describing triangles, rectangles, squares, and circles on index cards. For example, "I'm made with straight lines. I have 3 corners. I have 3 sides." Draw a shape on an index card to match each clue card. Make one clue card and one shape card for each student.
2. Tape a shape card to each student's back, hiding it from view. Give each student a matching clue card.
3. Have students read their clue cards to see if they can guess their shapes.
4. When students think they know their shapes, have them draw their guesses on the backs of their clue cards.
5. When all students finish, let them take off their shapes and see if they guessed correctly.

## Group 1 ○

**Real-World Shapes**

1. Explain to students that basic shapes can be seen in everyday objects.
2. Create a scavenger hunt and direct students to find at least three of each shape in the classroom. Have each student fold a sheet of 11" x 18" paper into fourths. Help students draw a different shape in each section and label each shape.
3. Instruct students to draw or list the items they find in the appropriate sections.
4. Challenge students to use these basic shapes to draw pictures of people or animals. Let students share the shapes they used to draw different body parts.

## Group 2 □

**Shape Sorting and Identification**

1. Have students sort geometric shape blocks by common attributes. Instruct each student to divide a sheet of 11" x 18" paper into fourths and label each section with a shape name: *triangle*, *rectangle*, *square*, and *circle*.
2. As students sort the shapes into the appropriate sections, ask, "Which shapes have straight sides? Which shapes have 4 sides? What do these shapes have in common? What's different about these shapes? Are these 2 shapes both triangles even though they are different sizes?"
3. When the shapes are sorted, let students trace several blocks in each section to create a poster of shapes.
4. Turn the papers over and challenge students to identify additional shapes in other categories: hexagons, octagons, trapezoids, and parallelograms.

## Group 3 △

**Shape Sorting with a Venn Diagram**

1. Have each student draw all of the shapes and cut them out of construction paper. Let students examine the shapes and brainstorm a list of attributes to describe the shapes, such as 4 sides, 3 corners, straight sides, etc.
2. Place two toy hoops on the table and overlap them slightly in the middle. Have students choose two attributes from their list and label each circle. For example, label one circle *4 sides* and one circle *straight sides*.
3. Have students place their shapes in the circles to sort them according to the attribute labels. Ask, "Do any shapes belong in the middle? Why? Do any shapes not belong in any section? Why?"
4. Repeat labeling the circles with different attributes. Encourage students to use correct vocabulary to talk about the similarities and differences between the shapes.

Name_____

Connect the dots to draw shapes.

Circles

Triangles

Squares

Rectangles

Name_____

Sort triangles, rectangles, squares, and circles in the table below.
Draw the shape or shapes that match each description.

| I have 3 sides. | I have 4 sides. | I do not have straight lines. |
|---|---|---|
|  |  |  |
| My sides have equal lengths. | My sides have different lengths. | My sides are parallel. |
|  |  |  |

Name_____

Cut out the shapes. Glue each shape into the correct part of the diagram.

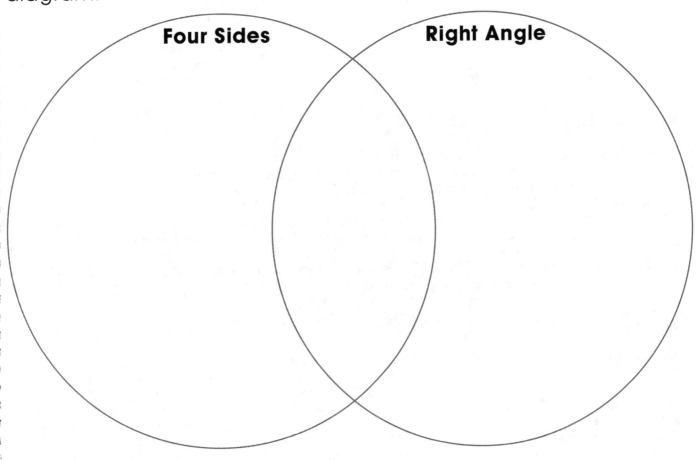

**Four Sides**          **Right Angle**

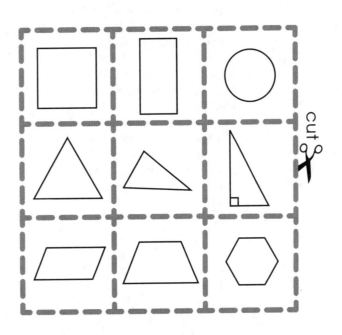

cut ✂

# Geometry

## Objective
Recognize and create two- and three-dimensional figures.

**Materials:**
- Large rubber balls
- Flying disks
- 2-D and 3-D figure examples (paper, shirt box, triangular sign, ice-cream cone, self-stick note, die, building blocks, etc.)
- Large paper bag
- Gumdrops
- Dehydrated fruit rolls
- Toothpicks
- Math notebooks
- Activity sheets (pages 75–77)

## Mini-Lesson

1. Introduce the difference between 2-D and 3-D figures by looking at a large rubber ball and a flying disk. Ask, "What is different about these two objects? What is the same?" Go outside and play with balls (spheres) and flying disks (circles). Ask students to compare how the figures move. For example, a ball rolls freely while a disk only rolls on its edge.
2. Return to the classroom and look at other 2-D and 3-D figures. Compare, for example, a rectangular sheet of paper with a shirt box, an ice-cream cone with a triangular sign, and a square self-stick note with a die.
3. Place the objects in a large paper bag.
4. Challenge students to carefully feel the objects inside the bag and identify each figure by touch. Have them tell each figure name and whether the figure is 2-D or 3-D.

## Group 1 ○

**Identifying Figures**
1. Have each student write 2-D and 3-D figure names along the side of a sheet of paper.
2. Challenge students to do a figure search in the classroom. To include all figures, scatter a few figure objects from the mini-lesson for students to find.
3. On their papers, students may draw or write the names of things they find beside the appropriate figure name. If students struggle reading the names, have them draw the figure beside each figure name before they begin the figure search.
4. Ask students to write a reflection in their math notebooks answering the prompt, "What is the difference between 2-D and 3-D?"

## Group 2 □

**Relating 2-D and 3-D Figures**
1. Provide a variety of 3-D figures (blocks or real-world items). Instruct students to examine the figures. Introduce the term *face* as a flat surface of a 3-D figure.
2. Have each student choose a 3-D figure and place it flat on one of its faces on a sheet of paper.
3. Instruct students to trace the face, remove the item, and see the resulting 2-D figure. Have them trace all of the faces for each 3-D figure. Ask, "What figures had square faces? Did any figures have more than 2 circular faces? Do any figures not have any faces?"
4. Ask students to write a reflection in their math notebooks answering the prompt, "How can 2-D figures be part of 3-D figures?"

## Group 3 △

**2-D and 3-D Building**
1. Provide each student with gumdrops and toothpicks.
2. Let students experiment with the gumdrops as vertices and the toothpicks as sides of 2-D figures. Ask, "Can you make a figure with just 2 gumdrops? Can you make a circle with these materials? Why or why not?"
3. Challenge students to use the materials to make 3-D figures. Ask, "How many gumdrops do you need to make a cube? How many toothpicks? Can you make a cone with these materials? Why or why not?"
4. Let students use dehydrated fruit rolls to create figures with curved surfaces.
5. Ask students to write a reflection in their math notebooks answering the prompt, "What does the *D* in 2-D and 3-D stand for? What are the 3 D's?"

Name_____

## Circle the name of each figure.

1.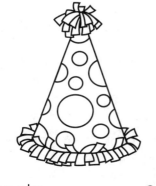

triangle          cone

2.

circle          cube

3.

cube          sphere

4.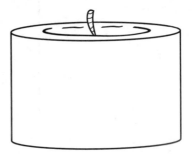

square          cylinder

5.

cylinder          rectangle

6.

sphere          circle

Name_____

Sort the 3-D figures from the figure bank in the table below. Draw or write the figure or figures that match each description.

| Figure Bank | | | |
| --- | --- | --- | --- |
| cylinder | cube | sphere | rectangular prism |
| triangular pyramid | | cone | square pyramid |

| I have 6 faces. | I have 2 or more square faces. | I do not have any faces. |
| --- | --- | --- |
| | | |
| I have at least one circular face. | I have 2 or more triangular faces. | I have 4 or fewer faces. |
| | | |

Name_____

Follow the clues to build or draw each figure. Write the name of the figure.

## 2-D Figures

1. I have 3 toothpicks and 3 gumdrops. What am I?

_____

2. I have 4 toothpicks and 4 gumdrops. What am I?

_____

3. I have 6 toothpicks and 6 gumdrops. What am I?

_____

4. I have no toothpicks or gumdrops. What am I?

_____

## 3-D Figures

5. I have 6 toothpicks and 4 gumdrops. What am I?

_____

6. I have 12 toothpicks and 8 gumdrops. What am I?

_____

7. I have 8 toothpicks and 5 gumdrops. What am I?

_____

8. I have no toothpicks or gumdrops. What could I be?

_____,_____,_____

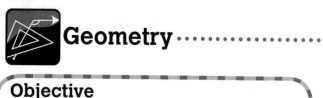

# Geometry

## Objective

Recognize and draw similar and congruent shapes.

**Materials:**
- Cardboard cutouts of similar and congruent shapes
- Small paper bags
- Assorted craft foam shapes
- Math notebooks
- Geoboards and rubber bands
- Dot paper
- Activity sheets (pages 79–81)

## Mini-Lesson

1. Hold up two different sizes of cardboard circles. Ask students to share what is the same about them: They are both circles, they are both round, and neither has any corners, etc. Then, ask students to share how they are different: They are different sizes. Explain that these circles are *similar*.
2. Hold up two identical circles and ask again, "What is the same and what is different?" Explain that things that are the same size and the same shape are called *congruent*.
3. Continue the activity with a variety of other shapes. Help students classify the shapes as similar or congruent.

## Group 1 ◯

**Congruency Game**

1. Give each student a paper bag with craft foam shapes inside and have pairs of students play a game.
2. Have each player reach into her bag, pull out a shape, and place it on the table. If the shapes are congruent, each player keeps her shape. If they are similar, the player with the larger shape keeps both shapes. If they are not alike at all, each player puts her shape back into her bag.
3. Play until all possible congruent and similar matches are made or until a time limit is met. The player with the most shapes (not including those still in his bag) is the winner.
4. Ask students to write a reflection in their math notebooks answering the prompt, "What does *similar* mean? What does *congruent* mean?"

## Group 2 ▢

**Making Similar and Congruent Shapes**

1. Have students create similar and congruent shapes using geoboards or dot paper.
2. Model a shape with a rubber band on a geoboard and have students make congruent shapes on their boards. Ask, "How are you sure your shape is congruent to my shape?"
3. Ask students to make a shape that is not congruent or similar to your shape.
4. Have students model a similar shape on their geoboards. This will likely be the hardest for students to do. Check that they are keeping the same shape proportions even though the sizes are different.
5. Let students experiment with other shapes like arrows, trapezoids, pentagons, etc. Let them turn their geoboards to see that the shapes do not change, even though they look different from different perspectives.
6. Ask students to write a reflection in their math notebooks answering the prompt, "Explain the difference between shapes that are similar and congruent."

## Group 3 △

**Transformed Shapes**

1. Show students two congruent squares, one oriented with a flat bottom and one oriented like a diamond. Ask, "Are these shapes similar or congruent? If they don't look the same, how can they be congruent?"
2. Show students two triangles, one equilateral triangle pointing to the right and one isosceles triangle pointing up. Ask, "These are both triangles turned in a different way. Are they congruent? Why or why not?"
3. Have students use dot paper to draw three pairs of congruent shapes where one shape in each pair is rotated a different way. Show students how to count the dots along the sides of the shapes to be sure the congruent pairs are the same size. Students may need to use shape blocks or cutouts as a reference for what the shapes should look like rotated.
4. Ask students to write a reflection in their math notebooks answering the prompt, "Can congruent shapes be similar? Can similar shapes be congruent?"

Name_____

Color each shape at the top a different color. Color congruent shapes matching colors.

**Shape Bank**

Name_____

Follow the directions to draw shapes. Use the dots as a guide.

1. Draw two congruent triangles.

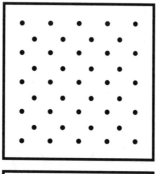

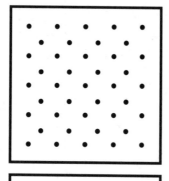

2. Draw two congruent rectangles.

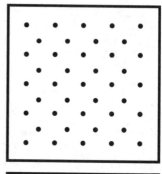

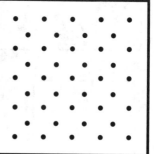

3. Draw two similar circles.

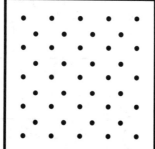

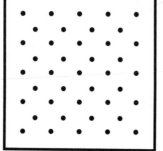

4. Draw two similar squares.

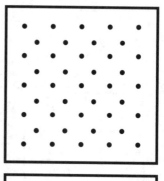

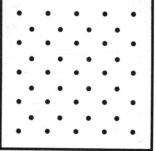

Name_____

In each row, circle each shape that is congruent with the first shape.

1.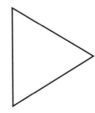

2.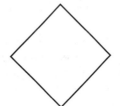

3.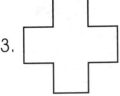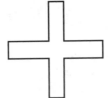

4.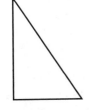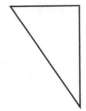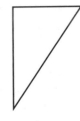

5.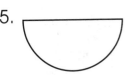

6.

# Data Analysis and Probability

## Objective
Sort objects and data by common attributes.

**Materials:**
- Toy hoops
- Circle cutouts
- Small paper plates
- Glue
- Large paper
- Math notebooks
- Activity sheets (pages 83–85)

## Mini-Lesson

1. Demonstrate a Venn diagram by letting students physically sort objects using toy hoops. Arrange two hoops side-by-side. Label one hoop *red* and one hoop *blue*. Provide several colorful circle cutouts: red, blue, and both red and blue.
2. Have students sort the circles in the hoops. Allow students to figure out what to do with the two-colored circles, prompting them to physically overlap the hoops.
3. Relabel the hoops *book* and *red*. Ask students to find objects in the classroom that could fit in the hoops: books, red objects, and red books. Show that if something is not red or a book, it stays outside the hoops.
4. Try other classifying combinations such as *blue/shoe* or *green/living*.

## Group 1 ○

**Attribute Sort**
1. Distribute copies of the activity sheet on page 83 and several small paper plates to each student. Have them color and cut out the buttons. Restrict students to using three colors.
2. Have students sort the buttons by size, color, shape, number of holes, etc., on the plates. Encourage them to label each plate to describe the attribute they used to sort.
3. Ask, "Can you sort the items using different attributes? Can you sort the items all into one category?" Let students practice sorting and resorting. Have them group their buttons with a partner's and sort together.
4. Ask students to write a reflection in their math notebooks answering the prompt, "What is an attribute?"

## Group 2 □

**Venn Diagram Sorting**
1. Distribute copies of the activity sheet on page 84. Have students color and cut out the bugs. Restrict students to using three colors.
2. Allow students time to decide how they would like to sort the bugs. Encourage them to consider color, size, length, number of legs, if it flies, etc.
3. Help students draw two overlapping circles to create Venn diagrams. Students should decide on two categories and label each circle in their diagrams.
4. Have students glue the bugs on their Venn diagrams in the appropriate sections.
5. Let students share their diagrams and discuss how their sorts are different or similar.
6. Ask students to write a reflection in their math notebooks answering the prompt, "How did you decide to sort the bugs using the Venn diagram? Could you have chosen different attributes?"

## Group 3 △

**Multiple Attributes**
1. Explain that glyphs are a pictorial form of data collection. Glyphs are often used by doctors to quickly record data about a patient. A dentist records cavities on a drawing of teeth, and a doctor marks injuries on a skeletal picture.
2. Have students complete the activity sheet on page 85. Display the glyphs and challenge students to create a triple Venn diagram with the collected data.
3. Show students how to create a triple Venn diagram on a large sheet of paper. Have them label the diagram with three attributes. For example, *girl, owns a dog*, and *6 years old*.
4. Direct each student to write his name in a section of the Venn diagram. Ask, "Which girls have a dog? In which section of the diagram did Michael write his name? Why?"
5. Ask students to write a reflection in their math notebooks answering the prompt, "How can a Venn diagram help you sort multiple attributes?"

Name_____

Color and cut out the buttons. Do not use more than 3 colors.

cut ✂

Name_____

Color and cut out the bugs. Do not use more than 3 colors.

cut ✂

Name_____

Follow the directions to color the glyph.

1. If you like dogs, color the dog's ears brown. If you like do not like dogs, color them black.

2. If you own a dog, color the nose pink. If you do not own a dog, color it black.

3. Draw a spot on the dog for every pet you own.

4. If you are a girl, color the dog bowl green. If you are a boy, color it orange.

5. Draw 1 whisker on the dog for every year you have been alive. For example, if you are 6 years old, draw 6 whiskers.

# Data Analysis and Probability

## Objective
Organize, represent, and compare data using graphs and charts.

**Materials:**
- Self-stick notes
- Straws
- Simple story or poem with repetitive words
- Collections of graphs from old magazines and newspapers
- Playing cards
- Crayons
- Math notebooks
- Activity sheets (pages 87–89)

## Mini-Lesson

1. Ask, "What pet is the class's favorite?" Discuss how you could collect the data. "Will it be easy to collect the data if everyone chooses a different pet? Why or why not?" Take some suggestions from the class and choose three or four pets to list horizontally on the board. Write the title *Favorite Pets*.
2. Collect the data by having each student place a self-stick note with her name in a column above the pet word on the board. Guide students to place their notes end to end so that the columns are even.
3. Discuss class results. Ask, "How do you know which animal was the class favorite and which was the least favorite?" Separate the notes in the least favorite pet column so that the top note is taller than the other columns. Ask, "Is this now the favorite pet? Why or why not?"
4. Use the class data to create a bar graph of the data. Draw bars around the self-stick notes and an axis.

## Group 1 ○

**Counting with Tallies**

1. Distribute straws and have students count them. Ask, "How could you count the straws faster and make it easier for another person to count them?"
2. Show students how they can quickly count the straws by fives using tallies. As with tallies, arrange four straws and then lay the fifth straw across. Ask, "How do you show a number that is not a multiple of 5?"
3. Let students practice writing tallies. Slowly read a story or a poem. Have students keep a tally of every time you say the word *the* or another common word in your text. Have students count their tallies and compare with the group.
4. Ask students to write a reflection in their math notebooks answering the prompt, "How can using tallies help you count faster?"

## Group 2 □

**Graphing Tally Data**

1. Let students look at collections of graphs from old magazines and newspapers and locate the following: titles, labels, keys, and data. Discuss the names of the types of graphs and charts and talk about what type of information each is useful for.
2. Hand random stacks of playing cards to pairs of students. Have one student flip over one card at a time while the other records hearts, spades, clubs, and diamonds in a tally chart. Ask, "If you didn't use tallies, what would be another way to keep track of the data?"
3. Have students use their tally charts to make simple bar graphs with the data. Ask, "How many bars will be in your graph? How will you label your graph? What suit did you have the most of? The least?"
4. Ask students to write a reflection in their math notebooks answering the prompt, "What is data, and how can I use it to create a graph?"

## Group 3 △

**Gathering and Comparing Data**

1. Have each student create a tally chart with the labels *red, blue, green, yellow, orange, purple, white,* and *black*.
2. Instruct students to look around the room and tally the colors of clothing items that their classmates are wearing. For example, if a student is wearing blue jeans and a white T-shirt, a tally would be marked for both blue and white.
3. Have each student use her data to create a bar graph of colors. Bars should be colored the labeled colors. Ask, "Which color was worn by most students today? How many more students wore blue than orange? Can you tell what the class's favorite color is from your data? Why or why not?"
4. Ask students to write a reflection in their math notebooks answering the prompt, "How can I use a graph to compare information?"

Name_____

Use tally marks to count the dots in each circle.

1.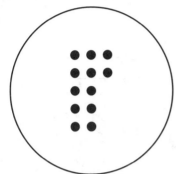

_____

2.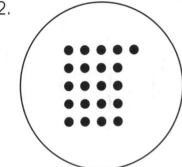

_____

3.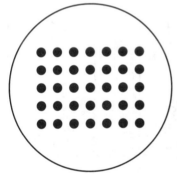

_____

Follow the directions.

4. Show 20 using tally marks. _____

5. Show 14 using tally marks. _____

6. Write the number shown.

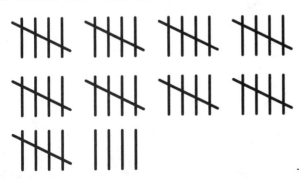

_____

Name_____

Ms. Garcia keeps stickers in her desk drawer. Count the stickers of each type to complete the tally chart. Use the data to draw a bar graph on the back of the page.

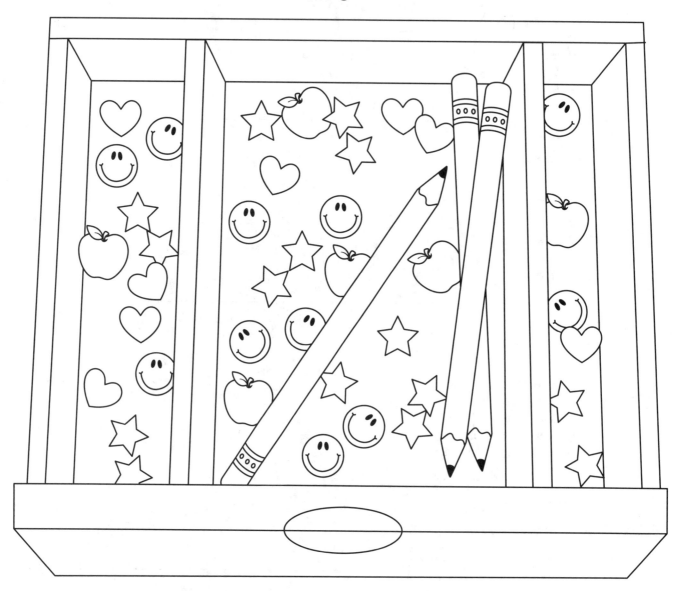

**Ms. Garcia's Stickers**

🍎

⭐

☺

♡

CD-104542 © Carson-Dellosa

Name_____

Students in Mr. Lee's class have many different types of shoes. Count the shoes of each type to complete the tally chart. Write a statement about the data. Use the data to draw a bar graph on the back of the page.

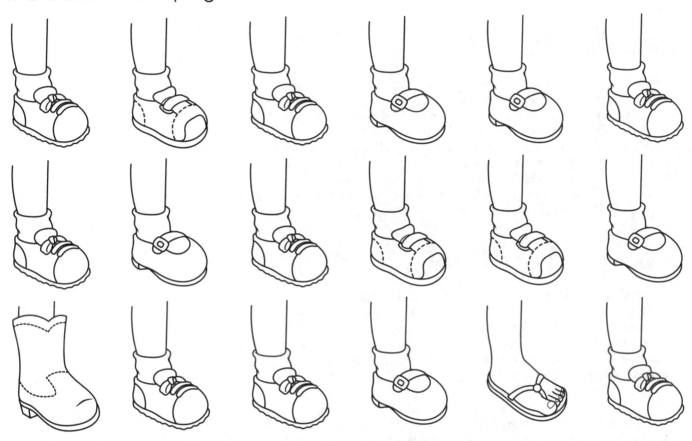

| Types of Shoes | |
|---|---|
| Laces | |
| Straps | |
| Buckles | |
| Other | |

I can tell from the data that _____

_____

_____

# Data Analysis and Probability

## Objective
Understand probability and predict outcomes.

**Materials:**
- Index cards
- Math notebooks
- Colorful marbles
- Paper bag
- Circle cutouts
- Crayons
- Activity sheets (pages 91–93)

## Mini-Lesson

1. Write the following vocabulary words on the board: *likely*, *unlikely*, *certain*, and *impossible*.
2. Talk about the difference between *likely* and *certain* and between *unlikely* and *impossible*. Discuss how unlikely things can possibly happen, but most likely will not happen. Ask students to think about what the qualifications are for something to be certain.
3. Encourage students to share things they feel will fall into each category. For example:
   Certain: The sun will set; the sun will rise.
   Likely: You will go to school on Monday; you will have homework today.
   Unlikely: You will go to Disney World next week; the mayor will visit your house.
   Impossible: A house will float into the sky on its own; a fish will walk on land.

## Group 1 ◯

### Likelihood in Literature

1. Continue the mini-lesson discussion. Give each student two index cards. Have each student label the sides of one card *certain* and *impossible* and the sides of the other card *likely* and *unlikely*.
2. Read a nursery rhyme such as "Hey, Diddle, Diddle," "Mary Had a Little Lamb," "Sing a Song of Sixpence," or "Hickory, Dickory, Dock."
3. As you read, have students lift their cards to show what parts of the rhymes are likely, unlikely, certain, or impossible. There will likely not be many "certain" responses, if any.
4. Ask students to write a reflection in their math notebooks answering the prompt, "What is the difference between certain and likely and between unlikely and impossible?"

## Group 2 ☐

### Predicting Likelihood

1. Empty a variety of marbles into a paper bag and ask a student volunteer to guess what color she will pick before reaching into the bag. Ask, "Was it easy to guess the color you would pick? Why or why not?"
2. Now, place only red marbles in the bag and ask another volunteer to guess the color of marble he will pick. Explain that picking a red marble is certain. Ask, "What is the chance of picking a yellow marble?"
3. Now, place only red and blue marbles in the bag, but use a lot more red than blue. Ask, "Which color are you likely to pick from the bag? Which color is unlikely? Is it certain you will pick a red marble? Why or why not? Is it impossible to pick a blue marble? A green marble?"
4. Ask students to write a reflection in their math notebooks answering the prompt, "How do I know when something is more likely to happen?"

## Group 3 △

### Creating Spinners

1. Show students a circle cutout that is divided equally in half with one side colored red and one side colored blue. Ask, "If this were a spinner, which color would you be more likely to spin?"
2. Show another circle divided equally into fourths with 3/4 red and 1/4 blue. Ask the same question and have students explain their thinking. Ask, "If you were playing a game where you win on a red spin and your opponent wins on a blue spin, which spinner would you rather play with? Which spinner would be fair to play with?"
3. Challenge students to create spinners to show a certain outcome for red, a likely outcome for red, an unlikely outcome for red, and an impossible outcome for red.
4. Ask students to write a reflection in their math notebooks answering the prompt, "What does *equally likely* mean?"

Name_____

Write whether each situation is likely, unlikely, certain, or impossible.

1. You will fly to Neptune tomorrow.

_____

2. You will go to school tomorrow.

_____

3. You will go to a party tomorrow.

_____

4. You will be 1 day older tomorrow.

_____

5. You will grow a tail tomorrow.

_____

6. You will see a bear tomorrow.

_____

7. You will see a dog tomorrow.

_____

8. You will be a human tomorrow.

_____

Name_____

## Circle each correct answer.

1.

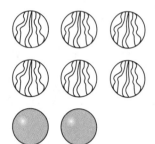

If you pick a marble without looking, which type are you likely to pick?

striped          solid

2.

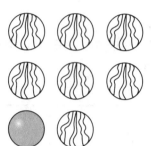

If you pick a marble without looking, which type are you unlikely to pick?

striped          solid

3.

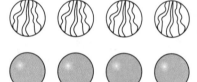

If you pick a marble without looking, which type are you certain to pick?

striped          solid          neither

4.

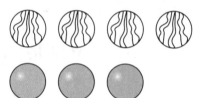

If you pick a marble without looking, which type is impossible to pick?

striped          solid          neither

5.

If you pick a marble without looking, which type are you certain to pick?

striped          solid          neither

6.

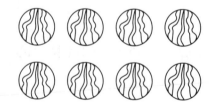

If you pick a marble without looking, which type is impossible to pick?

striped          solid          neither

**92**

Name_____

Look at each spinner. Decide if it is likely, unlikely, certain, or impossible to land on a shaded space.

1. 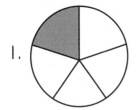 _____

2. 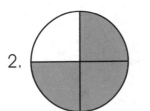 _____

3.  _____

4. 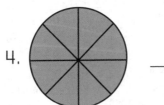 _____

Color each spinner to match its description.

5.

shaded outcome is likely

6.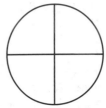

shaded outcome is impossible

7.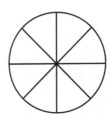

shaded outcome is certain

8.

shaded outcome is unlikely

# Answer Key

**Page 7**
1. 5; 2. 8; 3. 9; 4. 7; 5. 6 groups of 2 circles; 6. 6 groups of 3 circles; 7. 5 groups of 5 circles; 8. 5 groups of 4 circles

**Page 8**
1. 24; 2. 22; 3. 36; 4. 10 groups of 2 dots; 5. 7 groups of 5 dots; 6. 5 groups of 10 dots

**Page 9**
1. 50; 2. 64; 3. 71

**Page 11**
1. 1 ten 2 ones; 2. 0 tens 6 ones; 3. 2 tens 1 one; 4. 1 ten 9 ones; 5. 3 tens 4 ones; 6. 7 tens 0 ones; 7. 5 tens 7 ones; 8. 4 tens 2 ones; 9. 6 tens 3 ones; 10. 9 tens 5 ones

**Page 12**
1. 8 dimes 3 pennies; 2. 6 dimes 4 pennies; 3. 5 dimes 9 pennies; 4. 4 dimes 6 pennies; 5. 8 dimes 7 pennies; 6. 2 dimes 1 penny; 7. 3 dimes 8 pennies; 8. 7 dimes 0 pennies; 9. 9 dimes 3 pennies

**Page 13**
1. 45¢ + 31¢ = 76¢, 7 dimes 6 pennies; 2. 50¢ + 33¢ = 83¢, 8 dimes 3 pennies; 3. 31¢ + 15¢ = 46¢, 4 dimes 6 pennies; 4. 33¢ + 11¢ = 44¢, 4 dimes 4 pennies; 5. 24¢ + 12¢ = 36¢, 3 dimes 6 pennies; 6. 70¢ + 29¢ = 99¢, 9 dimes 9 pennies; 7. 29¢ + 15¢ = 44¢, 4 dimes 4 pennies; 8. 70¢ + 50¢ = 120¢ (or $1.20) 12 dimes 0 pennies

**Page 15**
1. 8; 2. 8; 3. 7; 4. 6; 5. 8; 6. 11; 7. 10; 8. 7; 9. 12; 10. 12

**Page 16**
Answers will vary.

**Page 17**
Answers will vary.

**Page 19**
1. 2, 4, 6, 8, 10, 12, 14, 16, 18, 20; 2. 5, 10, 15, 20, 25, 30, 35, 40, 45, 50; 3. 10, 20, 30, 40, 50, 60, 70, 80, 90, 100; 4. 20, 22, 24, 26, 28, 30, 32, 34, 36, 38; 5. 30, 35, 40, 45, 50, 55, 60, 65, 70, 75; 6. 30, 40, 50, 60, 70, 80, 90, 100, 110, 120; 7. Count by 2. 74, 76, 78, 80, 82, 84, 86, 88, 90, 92; 8. Count by 5. 15, 20, 25, 30, 35, 40, 45, 50, 55, 60

**Page 20**
1. 2, 4, 6, 8, 10, 12, 14, 16, 18, 20; 2. 5, 10, 15, 20, 25, 30, 35, 40, 45, 50; 3. 10, 20, 30, 40, 50, 60, 70, 80, 90, 100; 4. 52, 54, 56, 58, 60, 62, 64, 66, 68, 70; 5. 55, 60, 65, 70, 75, 80, 85, 90, 95, 100; 6. 1, 3, 5, 7, 9, 11, 13, 15, 17, 19; 7. Count by 5. 20, 25, 30, 35, 40, 45, 50, 55, 60, 65

**Page 21**
1. 20, 22, 24, 26, 28, 30, 32, 34, 36, 38, 40, even; 2. 5, 7, 9, 11, 13, 15, 17, 19, 21, 23, 25, odd; 3. 4, 9, 14, 19, 24, 29, 34, 39, 44, 49; 4. 8, 18, 28, 38, 48, 58, 68, 78, 88, 98; 5. 3, 6, 9, 12, 15, 18, 21, 24, 27, 30; 6. 4, 8, 12, 16, 20, 24, 28, 32, 36, 40; 7. 6, 12, 18, 24, 30, 36, 42; 8. 30, 45, 60, 75, 90, 105, 120

**Page 23**
Strips should be linked in rainbow order. The secret word is *CORRECT*.

**Page 24**
Patterns should be glued in ordinal order.

**Page 25**
The order of the pictures should be: dirty dog, get bucket, fill bucket, add soap, lather dog, rinse dog, dog shakes, dry dog, brush dog, hug dog.

**Page 27**
1. 1, 2, 3, 4, 5, 6, 7, 8, 8¢; 2. 25, 50, 75, 100, 100¢ or $1.00; 3. 10, 20, 30, 40, 50, 60, 70, 70¢; 4. 5, 10, 15, 20, 25, 30, 30¢; 5. 5, 10, 15, 20, 25, 30, 35, 40, 40¢; 6. 25, 50, 75, 100, 125, 125¢ or $1.25

**Page 28**
1. 25 + 1 + 1 + 1 + 1 + 1 = 30¢; 2. 1 + 5 + 1 + 1 + 1 + 1 = 10¢; 3. 1 + 1 + 1 + 1 + 1 + 1 = 6¢; 4. 10 + 1 + 5 + 1 + 1 + 1 + 1 = 20¢; 5. 5 + 1 + 1 + 1 + 25 + 1 + 1 + 1 = 36¢; 6. 5 + 1 + 1 + 1 + 1 + 1 + 5 + 1 + 5 = 21¢; 7. 5 + 10 + 1 + 1 + 5 + 10 + 1 + 1 + 1 + 1 = 36¢; 8. Answers will vary.

**Page 29**
Possible answers: 1. 1 penny, 0 nickels, 0 dimes, 3 quarters or 1 penny, 1 nickel, 2 dimes, 2 quarters; 2. 0 pennies, 1 nickel, 0 dimes, 2 quarters or 5 pennies, 0 nickels, 5 dimes, 0 quarters; 3. 4 pennies, 0 nickels, 2 dime, 3 quarters or 4 pennies, 1 nickel, 9 dimes, 0 quarters; 4. 2 pennies, 0 nickels, 1 dime, 1 quarter or 2 pennies, 1 nickel, 3 dimes, 0 quarters; 5. 4 pennies, 0 nickels, 1 dime, 2 quarters or 4 pennies, 1 nickel, 3 dimes, 1 quarter; 6. 0 pennies, 0 nickels, 0 dimes, 5 quarters or 5 pennies, 0 nickels, 2 dimes, 4 quarters

**Page 31**
1. Beads should follow an ABB pattern. 2. Beads should follow an AB pattern. 3. Beads should follow an AAB pattern. 4. AB, round; 5. ABB, striped; 6. AAB, heart

**Page 32**
1. Beads should follow an AB pattern. 2. Beads should follow an ABB pattern. 3. Beads should follow an ABC pattern. 4. AABB, first 4 beads should be circled, beads should follow an AABB pattern. 5. ABC, first 3 beads should be circled, beads should follow an ABC pattern. 6. ABA, first 3 beads should be circled, beads should follow an ABA pattern.

**Page 33**
Patterns will vary but should follow the pattern descriptions.

**Page 35**
1. −, 3; 2. +, 8; 3. −, 2; 4. −, 10; 5. +, 5

**Page 36**
1. 3 + 3 = 6, 6 − 3 = 3; 2. 4 + 1 = 5, 5 − 1 = 4; 3. 2 + 4 = 6, 6 − 4 = 2; 4. 5 + 3 = 8, 8 − 3 = 5; 5. 3 + 2 = 5, 5 − 2 = 3; 6. 5 + 4 = 9, 9 − 5 = 4

**Page 37**
2. 5 + 2 = 7, 9 − 2 = 7; 3. 8 − 3 = 5, 2 + 3 = 5; 4. 7 − 4 = 3, 10 − 7 = 3; 5. 9 + 0 = 9 or 9 − 0 = 9, 5 + 4 = 9; 6. 0 + 6 = 6, 8 − 2 = 6

**Page 40**
Answers will vary.

# Answer Key

## Page 41
1. 10 − 3 + 6 = 13 cookies; 2. 8 + 4 − 5 − 2 = 5 cookies; 3. 15 − 9 − 3 + 7 + 5 = 15 cookies; 4. 12 + 8 − 5 + 2 − 10 = 7 cookies; 5. 13 − 9 + 2 + 7 − 4 = 9 cookies

## Page 43
1. all cars red; 2. 9 cars red, 1 car blue, 1 + 9 = 10, 10 − 1 = 9, 10 − 9 = 1; 3. 8 cars red, 2 cars blue, 2 + 8 = 10, 10 − 2 = 8, 10 − 8 = 2; 4. 7 cars red, 3 cars blue, 7 + 3 = 10, 3 + 7 = 10, 10 − 3 = 7, 10 − 7 = 3; 5. 6 cars red, 4 cars blue, 6 + 4 = 10, 4 + 6 = 10, 10 − 6 = 4, 10 − 4 = 6; 6. 5 cars red, 5 cars blue, 5 + 5 = 10, 10 − 5 = 5

## Page 44
1. 6 + 4 = 10, 4 + 6 = 10, 10 − 6 = 4, 10 − 4 = 6; 2. 8 + 6 = 14, 6 + 8 = 14, 14 − 8 = 6, 14 − 6 = 8; 3. 7 on top of triangle, 4 + 3 = 7, 3 + 4 = 7, 7 − 4 = 3, 7 − 3 = 4; 4. 12 on top of triangle, 8 + 4 = 12, 4 + 8 = 12, 12 − 8 = 4, 12 − 4 = 8; 5. 15 on top of triangle, 6 + 9 = 15, 9 + 6 = 15, 15 − 9 = 6, 15 − 6 = 9; 6. 18 on top of triangle, 9 + 9 = 18, 18 − 9 = 9; 7. 3 in corner of triangle, 7 + 3 = 10, 3 + 7 = 10, 10 − 7 = 3, 10 − 3 = 7; 8. 3 in corner of triangle, 5 + 3 = 8, 3 + 5 = 8, 8 − 5 = 3, 8 − 3 = 5

## Page 45
1. 6 in corner of triangle, 5 + 6 = 11, 6 + 5 = 11, 11 − 5 = 6, 11 − 6 = 5; 2. 7 in corner of triangle, 9 + 7 = 16, 7 + 9 = 16, 16 − 9 = 7, 16 − 7 = 9; 3. 9 in corner of triangle, 4 + 9 = 13, 9 + 4 = 13, 13 − 9 = 4, 13 − 4 = 9; 4. 8 in corner of triangle, 8 + 2 = 10, 2 + 8 = 10, 10 − 8 = 2, 10 − 2 = 8; 5. Answers will vary. 6. Answers will vary.

## Page 47
1. <; 2. <; 3. <; 4. >; 5. >; 6. <; 7. >; 8. <; 9. Answers will vary. 10. Answers will vary.

## Page 48
1. 91; 2. 17; 3. 26; 4. 80; 5. 72; 6. 39 or 33; 7. 49; 8. 55; 9. 39 or 33; 10. 64

## Page 49
Possible answers: 1. 46 > 10; 2. 95 > 32; 3. 81 < 83; 4. 70 > 40; 5. 52 < 93; 6. 57 > 48; 7. 59 < 60; 8. 82 > 71

## Page 51

## Page 52
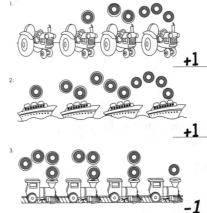

## Page 53
1. 0, 1, 2, 3, 4, 5, 6; 2. 7, 6, 5, 4, 3, 2, 1; 3. 12, 13, 14, 15, 16, 17, 18; 4. 3, 5, 7, 9, 11, 13, 15; 5. 60, 70, 80, 90, 100, 110, 120; 6. +5, 5, 10, 15, 20, 25, 30, 35; 7. Answers will vary.

## Page 55
Answers will vary.

## Page 56
1. 3 cubes; 2. 7 cubes; 3. 5 cubes; 4. 2 cubes; 5. 6 cubes

## Page 57
1. 3 small, 2 large; 2. 4 small, 3 large; 3. 5 small, 4 large; 4. more; Answers will vary. 5. Answers will vary.

## Page 59
1. bathroom scale; 2. cm ruler; 3. thermometer; 4. grocer's scale; 5. tape measure; 6. grocer's scale; 7. pan balance; 8. in. ruler

## Page 60
1. 3 centimeters; 2. 6 feet; 3. 20 ounces; 4. 1 millimeter; 5. 450 kilograms; 6. 10 inches; 7. 7 centimeters; 8. 100 yards

## Page 61
1. 3 inches; 2. 6 inches; 3. 1 inch; 4. 4 inches; 5. 2 inches

## Page 63
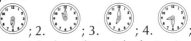
1. ; 2. ; 3. ; 4. ; 5. two o'clock; 6. five o'clock; 7. nine thirty or half past nine; 8. twelve thirty or half past twelve

## Page 64
1. 9:30; 2. 12:00; 3. 7:00; 4. 4:30; 5.–8. Answers will vary.

## Page 65
3, 8:00 A.M.; 6, 12:30 P.M.; 7, 3:00 P.M.; 1, 7:00 A.M.; 5, 10:00 A.M.; 2, 7:30 A.M.; 4, 8:30 A.M.; 10, 10:00 P.M.; 9, 6:30 P.M.; 8, 4:30 P.M.

## Page 67
1. over; 2. through or between; 3. above; 4. next to or beside; 5. behind; 6. in front of

## Page 68

## Page 69
Answers will vary.

## Page 71
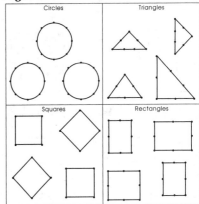

# Answer Key

## Page 72

| I have 3 sides. | I have 4 sides. | I do not have straight lines. |
|---|---|---|
| ▲ | ■ (square above rectangle) | ● |
| **My sides have equal lengths.** | **My sides have different lengths.** | **My sides are parallel.** |
| ■ above ▲ | ▲ (triangle) | ■ above ▬ (rectangle) |

## Page 73

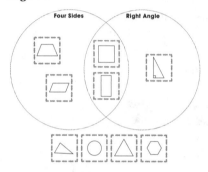

## Page 75

1. cone; 2. circle; 3. cube; 4. cylinder;
5. rectangle; 6. sphere

## Page 76

| I have 6 faces. | I have 2 or more square faces. | I do not have any faces. |
|---|---|---|
| cube above rectangular prism | cube above rectangular prism | sphere |
| **I have circle faces.** | **I have 2 or more triangle faces.** | **I have 4 or fewer faces.** |
| cylinder above cone | square pyramid above triangular pyramid | cylinder, cone, triangular pyramid, sphere |

## Page 77

1. triangle; 2. square; 3. hexagon;
4. circle; 5. triangular pyramid;
6. cube; 7. square pyramid; 8. sphere, cone, or cylinder

## Page 79

Congruent shapes should be colored the same.

## Page 80

Appropriate shapes should be drawn.

## Page 81

1. circle 3rd and 4th shapes; 2. circle 2nd and 4th shapes; 3. circle 3rd and 4th shapes; 4. circle all shapes;
5. circle 3rd and 4th shapes; 6. circle 4th shape

## Page 85

Answers will vary.

## Page 87

1. 12 tally marks; 2. 21 tally marks;
3. 35 tally marks; 4. 20 tally marks;
5. 14 tally marks; 6. 49

## Page 88

Tally marks in the chart: 6 apples, 15 stars, 11 smiley faces, 8 hearts

## Page 89

Tally marks in the chart: 8 laces, 3 straps, 5 buckles, 2 other

## Page 91

1. impossible; 2. likely; 3. unlikely;
4. certain; 5. impossible; 6. unlikely;
7. likely (or unlikely or certain depending on situation); 8. certain

## Page 92

1. striped; 2. solid; 3. neither;
4. neither; 5. striped; 6. solid

## Page 93

1. unlikely; 2. likely; 3. impossible;
4. certain; 5. Possible answer:

6.  ; 7.

8. Possible answer: